ISD
INSTRUCTIONAL SYSTEMS DESIGN

Robert R. Carkhuff and
Sharon G. Fisher

with

John R. Cannon,
Theodore W. Friel, and
Richard M. Pierce

Human Resource Development Press, Inc.
Publishers of Human Technology

Copyright © 1984 by
Human Resource Development Press, Inc.

22 Amherst Rd.
Amherst, Massachusetts 01002 (413) 253-3488

Bernice R. Carkhuff, Publisher

First Edition, First printing, January, 1984
          Second printing, August, 1984

Library of Congress Cataloging in Publication Data
International Standard Book Number 0-914234-71-4

Cover Art by Krawczyk
Cover Design by Tom Bellucci
Composition by Jean Miller
Printing and Binding by Bookcrafters, Inc.

TABLE OF CONTENTS

About The Authors

Robert R. Carkhuff, Ph.D., Chairman, Carkhuff Institute of Human Technology, Amherst, Massachusetts, is among the most-cited social scientists according to the Institute for Scientific Information. He is author of three of the most-referenced social science texts, including two volumes on *"Helping and Human Relations."* His latest books are *"Sources of Human Productivity"* and *"The Exemplary Performer in the Age of Productivity."*

Sharon G. Fisher, M.Ed., Director, Instructional Systems Design, Human Technology, Inc., McLean, Virginia, has designed hundreds of public and private sector instructional projects and products. She is recipient of the first "Exemplar Award" for her exemplary products in C.A.I. as well as print material.

John R. Cannon, Ph.D., Director Management Systems, Human Technology, Inc., McLean, Virginia, has directed more than 600 projects in the last 12 years. He is co-author of a forthcoming book on *"The Art and Science of Consulting."*

Richard M. Pierce, Ph.D., Director, Human Resource Development, Human Technology, Inc., McLean, Virginia, has designed the implementation programs for more than 500 projects in the last 15 years. He is co-author of a forthcoming book on *"Performance Management Systems."*

Theodore W. Friel, Ph.D., Director Advanced Systems Design, Human Technology, Inc., McLean, Virginia, has done operations planning for more than 400 projects in the last 14 years. He is author of *"The Art of Developing a Career"* and co-author of a forthcoming book on *"Human Resource Planning."*

Preface

The era of "quick and dirty" training programs is over. The Age of Productivity demands outcome for every training dollar invested.

Training evaluations which suggest that "everyone liked it" will no longer satisfy decision makers nor protect the jobs of training personnel.

The keys to effective training outcomes are a systematically-developed instructional design and a systematically-implemented training delivery.

ISD was developed with and for professionals in the training and development community. More and more of these professionals are realizing that instructional design must be directly derived from the mission and goal needs of the target organization. More and more of these professionals are realizing that their instructional interventions will be judged according to their contribution to organizational and individual productivity.

Volume I of ISD presents the tools that training and development professionals need to design productivity-focused instructional interventions. These tools are organized within the following major tasks:
- Establishing Productivity Goals
- Analyzing Contextual Tasks
- Specifying Training Objectives
- Developing Training Content
- Planning Training Delivery

Together with Volume II, *Evaluating Instructional Systems,* ISD responds to the needs and challenges of the professional training and development community. It is to these professionals that we dedicate these efforts.

R.R.C.
S.G.F.

Washington, D.C.
January 1984

Foreword

Robert R. Carkhuff and his associates are to human processing what Jack Kilby and his associates were to computer processing. Kilby brought us the microprocessor and, in so doing, introduced the Age of Information Processing. Carkhuff brought us training and learning strategies and, in so doing, introduced the Age of Human Productivity.

We in information processing have long recognized the need for "thinking humans" to drive our information systems. Now we have the vehicles for training the thinking humans. Moreover, now we have the vehicles for transforming their thought processes into organizational productivity.

Carkhuff, Fisher, Cannon, Friel, and Pierce bring us the distillation of their own processing on instructional systems design. Beginning with the missions of the decision-makers, they teach us how to transform these missions into measurable productivity improvements. Volume I provides us with the skills of designing instructional systems. Volume II offers us the skills of evaluating instructional systems. Together, they provide a comprehensive picture of the place of education and training in productivity systems design.

The models, systems, and skills are not only totally innovative and fluidly communicative, they are also presented in an information-simplified manner, with abundant job aids and illustrations. The authors demonstrate the power of their own productivity in their products. They have given order and potency to a once-chaotic area.

The core of *ISD* remains the operations at the various stations. In Volume I, the authors teach us how to analyze tasks, define training objectives, and develop content and training plans. In Volume II, they teach us how to use a criterion-referenced approach to evaluation. Their mode of teaching is highly operational and highly useful. Above all, it is logical, simple and straight-forward.

These *ISD* volumes enable us to make a multitude of applications in our daily operations in the private sector. No longer do we require six months to design a training program that is already obsolete. We can now make immediate contributions to immediate needs. To be sure, we can design instructional systems to achieve any human goal in business or government or, for that matter, in our homes and in our schools.

To sum, these two volumes on instructional design teach us how to transform the smallest value in a decision-maker's head into a productive training delivery. They are a necessary resource for every manager of human resources and every developer and deliverer of education and training.

In short, Carkhuff and his associates teach us that we get what we train for—no more, no less! Our training productivity will be as productive as our instructional design is systematic. These volumes teach us how to develop and evaluate these systematic designs. *ISD* is clearly the most systematic approach to training design.

Jack Kelly
Manager, Human Resources
Information Systems Technology Group
International Business Machines

INTRODUCTION

THE PRODUCTIVE INTERVENTION: A CASE STUDY

An Industrial Relations (IR) Department of a multinational corporation was responsible for productivity improvement through human and information resource development. IR policy makers established a new mission of providing productivity improvement services throughout the corporation. In other words:

EXTERNAL MISSION: To market and deliver productivity improvement services to other Departments within the corporation and other corporations.

CONSULTING DESIGN

The expansion of the IR Department's mission was viewed as an R & D effort. A special cost center was established for tracking the costs and benefits generated by the productivity improvement program (PIP). To gain full corporate acceptance of PIP, it was essential that the IR Department prepare its own personnel for such a mission. In other words, IR needed to improve the performance of its individual personnel and the overall productivity of its own Department in order to be successful.

INTERNAL MISSION: To improve the performance of IR consultants.

The burden of the performance improvement efforts falls upon the resource component within IR. The strategic goal was to improve the performance of IR resources while reducing the resource expenditures.

STRATEGIC GOAL: To increase individual IR staff performance outcomes by 10%, while reducing resource expenditures by 5%.

IR's resource component needed to make strategic decisions concerning the alternative courses of actions to be used in order to reach the strategic goal. Basically, IR had to choose between increasing its internal capacity through hiring and firing or developing its internal capacity through training. Employing the productivity values of the policy makers, the IR resource component decided that developing its internal capacity was the most cost beneficial course of action.

STRATEGIC DECISION: To develop the internal consulting capacity through personnel training.

Accordingly, strategic plans were developed for implementing the selected course of action. The strategic plans detailed the instructional design tasks to be performed.

STRATEGIC PLANS: To develop instructional systems design to train IR personnel.

INSTRUCTIONAL DESIGN

The strategic plan was delivered to the decision makers. After consideration, the decision makers refined the plan by recycling the strategic decisions, goals, and mission. The instructional system design (ISD) was initiated by establishing the productivity goals for the personnel to be trained.

ISD PRODUCTIVITY   To improve the quantity and quality of individual
GOAL: consulting performance by 10% or more.

In order to improve individual performance, the instructional technologist needed to analyze the tasks that the personnel would be required to perform. This analysis emphasized the processing of the inputs into outputs. It also included the enabling tasks that overcame the barriers to the performance of process tasks.

PERSONNEL TASKS: To process consulting inputs more efficiently and consulting outputs more effectively.

The training objectives emphasized the skills the personnel needed in order to perform their consulting tasks more productively. The objectives emphasized the skills that underlie planning, producing, and assessing tasks. These skills became the training objectives.

TRAINING   To apply skills underlying planning, producing, and
OBJECTIVES: assessing to consulting tasks.

The training content flowed directly from the training objective. It emphasized the skill steps and supportive knowledge which the personnel would require to perform the planning, producing, and assessing skills.

CONTENT OUTCOMES: To acquire the skill steps and supportive knowledge required to perform the planning, producing, and assessing skills.

A training delivery plan was developed. It organized the training content to facilitate the training delivery. It emphasized the training methods that insured learning.

DELIVERY OUTCOMES: To organize the content and methods to insure trainee learning.

Finally, the training delivery was made. The trainers emphasized both the requirements of the content and the experiences of the trainees in making the training delivery. The ISD personnel now needed to assess the efficacy of their training delivery. They assessed it at several different levels of process and outcome.

PROCESS ASSESSMENT: Did the trainees give evidence of receiving the training delivery?

Given that the trainees received the training delivery, the question concerning whether they acquired the training content remained.

ACQUISITION ASSESSMENT: Did the trainees acquire the planning, producing, and assessing skills content?

Given that the trainees acquired the content, it was still necessary to inquire into their ability to apply the skills to the training objective.

APPLICATION ASSESSMENT: Did the trainees apply their skills to the planning, producing, and assessing objectives?

The more relevant question concerning the transfer of the skills to real-life tasks remained.

TRANSFER ASSESSMENT: Did the trained personnel transfer their skills to real-life consulting tasks?

Finally, the ISD personnel want to know whether they achieved their original goals.

ACHIEVEMENT ASSESSMENT: Did the trained personnel improve the quantity and quality of their individual consulting performance by 10%?

In turn, these assessments were related to the original strategic goals flowing from the internal mission.

STRATEGIC GOAL: Did the trained personnel increase their results outputs while reducing their resource inputs?

INSTRUCTIONAL EVALUATION

All of these stages of a productive intervention were developed and implemented. Upon process assessment, it was found that all of the trainees gave demonstrable evidence of receiving the training delivery: <u>the trainees produced their own individual learning programs</u>.

> **PROCESS RESULTS:** On 5-point scales, the trainees were rated at 4.7 in terms of their movement toward acting to receive the training delivery.

Acquisition assessments yielded similarly positive ratings: <u>the trainees acquired the skill steps and knowledge of the training content</u>.

> **ACQUISITION RESULTS:** On 5-point scales, the trainees were rated at 4.7 in terms of their performance of the skills.

Similarly, application assessments produced positive results: <u>the trainees applied their skills to the training objectives simulating the real-life work tasks</u>.

> **APPLICATION RESULTS:** On 5-point scales, the trainees were rated at 4.5 in terms of applying their skills to the training objectives.

Also, the assessments of transfer yielded positive results: <u>the trained personnel transferred their skills to their consulting tasks</u>.

> **TRANSFER RESULTS:** On 5-point scales, personnel were rated at 4.7 in terms of using their skills in everyday consulting tasks.

Finally, the goal achievement yielded positive results: <u>the personnel improved their performance in consulting</u>.

> **ACHIEVEMENT RESULTS:** The personnel were able to improve the quantity and quality of their performance by more than 10%.

Thus, the ISD intervention was successful in achieving its personnel performance goals. It remained to relate the ISD goals to the strategic goals and the original mission.

The success of the ISD intervention was instrumental in achieving the strategic goals.

> **STRATEGIC GOAL**   The organizational output increased by 25% while the
> **RESULTS:**   resource expenditures were reduced by 16%.

Thus, by intervening with an instructional design derived systematically from its strategic goals, the IR Department was able to surpass its goals and achieve its internal mission. IR was now prepared to address its external mission, that of expanding its services throughout the entire corporation.

In summary, productive interventions begin with measurable goals derived systematically from effective policy. Where appropriate, productive interventions may end with measurable goals achieved systematically through instructional intervention. In short, instructional systems design is a vehicle for achieving desirable individual performance and organizational productivity goals through systematic intervention.

In the pages that follow, an overview of the consulting intervention process will be presented. This overview is followed by an elaboration on the details of the stations of productive instructional interventions. In comprehensive productivity system designs, instructional designs may be a necessary ingredient to productivity improvement. Basically, you get what you train for--no more, no less! If your design is comprehensive and systematic, you may achieve tangible productivity benefits as did the IR Department in the case study. If your design is not comprehensive and systematic, you may place yourself and your organization in jeopardy.

Work--as life--in the Age of Information--is as productive as its implementers are systematic in processing its data. For instructional technologists, processing the data inputs of the decision makers and transforming them into the performance improvements of trained personnel is part of the job.

CONSULTING INTERVENTION OVERVIEW

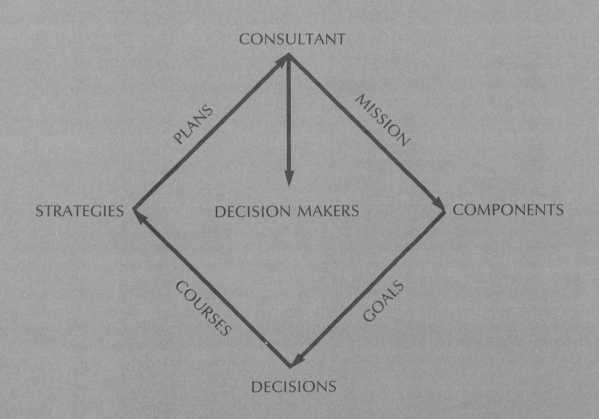

> **ALL EFFECTIVE INSTRUCTIONAL DESIGN IS
> PRECEDED BY A CONSULTING INTERVENTION**

**What Is A
Consulting
Intervention?**

The purpose of a consulting intervention is to refine the productivity mission so that strategic plans can be developed. A comprehensive consulting intervention includes the following stages:

- STAGE 1: Formulating the Mission
- STAGE 2: Developing Strategic Goals
- STAGE 3: Selecting Preferred Courses of Action
- STAGE 4: Developing Strategic Plans
- STAGE 5: Making the Strategic Delivery
- STAGE 6: Evaluating the Consulting Processes

**Who Conducts
The Consulting
Intervention?**

Most instructional design personnel are not directly involved in the consulting intervention. Typically, policy makers or their representatives such as the Chief Executive Officers (CEO's) initiate the consulting intervention. Increasingly, with the information demands of the Information Age, these executive officers will have external or internal consultants guide them through the consulting intervention.

**Why Is The
Consulting
Intervention
Important?**

The information generated during the consulting intervention is a precondition for instructional design. Instructional design personnel must be aware of the consulting intervention even if they are not directly involved in the process. Beginning the instructional design intervention without the information generated during the consulting intervention is similar to going out to sea without a compass or other navigational devices.

What If Consulting Has Not Occurred?

If a consulting intervention has not been conducted, then the instructional designers should work with policy makers to formulate the mission, develop strategic goals, make strategic decisions, and develop strategic plans. However, there may be situations where working with policy makers is out of the question. Under these circumstances, the instructional designers should patch together the consulting intervention information through existing documents and other sources.

> **REMEMBER . . .**
>
> Don't proceed with the instructional design intervention until you have your bearings.

STAGE 1: FORMULATING THE MISSION

What Is A Productivity Mission?

A productivity mission is simply a statement of goals for different target populations. Target populations may be either <u>external</u> or <u>internal</u> to the organization. Often, goals for external target populations, such as customers, have implications for internal target populations, such as managers.

MISSION = GOALS x TARGET POPULATIONS
. External
. Internal

How Is The Mission Formulated?

The mission is formulated by first identifying the target populations. Next, goals are established for the target populations. The goals are usually stated in terms of results outputs and/or resource inputs:

$$\frac{\text{RESULTS OUTPUTS (RO)}}{\text{RESOURCE INPUTS (RI)}}$$

Ideally, goals attempt to improve results outputs while reducing resource inputs. A productivity mission would therefore be:

$$\frac{\text{RO +}}{\text{RI -}}$$

Examples

Table 1 presents examples of types of goals for external and internal target populations.

Table 1.

EXAMPLES OF TYPES OF GOALS BY TARGET POPULATIONS

TARGET POPULATIONS

	EXTERNAL	INTERNAL
RESULTS IMPROVEMENT	• Using new and more powerful resources. • Producing new and more profitable products. • Segmenting new and more profitable markets. • Developing universal methods of distributing.	• Increasing critical personnel, information, and capital resources. • Increasing production output. • Increasing market share. • Increasing distribution.
RESOURCE REDUCTION	• Reducing old and more expensive resources. • Reducing old and unprofitable products. • Reducing old and unprofitable markets. • Reducing archaic distribution methods.	• Reducing capital expenditures for materials, methods, equipment, energy, and space. • Reducing production expenditures. • Reducing marketing expenditures. • Reducing distribution expenditures.

What If The Ideal Is Not Possible?

Most often, ideal productivity missions (i.e., $\frac{RO\ +}{RI\ -}$) are not possible. Frequently, it is necessary to make resource expenditures in order to increase results outputs. For example, we may be willing to invest resources in recruiting or training personnel in order to increase their performance. In these cases, we may compare the increments in results with the cost expenditures. We call this comparison an analysis of return-on-investment (ROI).

$$ROI \quad = \quad \frac{\underline{RESULTS\ INCREMENTS}}{RESOURCE\ EXPENDITURES}$$

What Are Other Types Of Missions?

In reality, productivity missions may involve increasing, decreasing, or maintaining either results outputs or resource inputs. We may even increase resources in order to slow down the short-term deterioration of results outputs.

TYPE OF MISSION	Results Outputs	Resource Inputs
Increasing		
Decreasing		
Maintaining		

Instructional designers must know which cell(s) in the above matrix are operating within their organization's productivity mission. The instructional design must be synchronized with the productivity mission.

Summary

The productivity mission is simply a statement of goals for different target populations, both external customers/ clients and internal personnel. The productivity mission emphasizes a comparison of results outputs with the resource inputs.

$$PRODUCTIVITY\ MISSION \quad = \quad \frac{\underline{RESULTS\ OUTPUTS}}{RESOURCE\ INPUTS}$$

The goals of a productivity mission may emphasize increasing, decreasing, or maintaining either the results outputs or the resource inputs.

CONSULTANT

MISSION

```
┌─────────────────────────────────────────────────────┐
│                                                       │
│        STAGE 2:   DEVELOPING STRATEGIC GOALS          │
│                                                       │
└─────────────────────────────────────────────────────┘
```

**What Are
Strategic
Goals?**

Strategic goals are those which support the achievement of a productivity mission. Our strategic goals tell us what the organization must do in order to achieve the productivity mission.

**How Are
Strategic
Goals
Developed?**

Once a productivity mission has been formulated, then an analysis of the organization's strategic components is conducted. Strategic components are the organizational units which share in the achievement of the mission. Strategic components usually include the following organizational units:

```
┌─────────────────────────────────────────────────────┐
│                                                       │
│        •    Resource Component                        │
│        •    Production Component                       │
│        •    Marketing Component                        │
│        •    Distribution Component                     │
│                                                       │
└─────────────────────────────────────────────────────┘
```

During the consulting analysis, each strategic component is analyzed. The analysis yields refined goals for any one or more of the critical components.

Examples

Table 2 presents examples of types of strategic goals that can be developed for each organizational component.

Summary

Strategic goals tell us what the organizational components must do in order to achieve the productivity mission. Instructional designers must fully understand the strategic goals developed for the organizational components (i.e., resource, production, marketing, distribution) within which they are working. The instructional intervention must support the strategic goals.

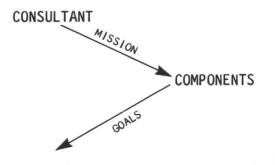

Table 2.

EXAMPLES OF TYPES OF STRATEGIC GOALS

ORGANIZATIONAL COMPONENTS	EXAMPLE		
RESOURCE	GOAL	=	$\dfrac{\text{Improve Resource Capacity (+ 20\%)}}{\text{Limit Resource Expenditures (+ 10\%)}}$
PRODUCTION	GOAL	=	$\dfrac{\text{Improve Production Outputs (+ 5\%)}}{\text{Maintain Production Expenditures}}$
MARKETING	GOAL	=	$\dfrac{\text{Improve Market Share (+ 50\%)}}{\text{Limit Marketing Expenditures (+ 25\%)}}$
DISTRIBUTION	GOAL	=	$\dfrac{\text{Improve Distribution (+ 25\%)}}{\text{Reduce Distribution (- 10\%)}}$

NOTE: Similar to the productivity mission, strategic goals usually emphasize improving results outputs. Resource expenditures may or may not be reduced. It may be necessary to make resource investments, such as training, in order to increase the results outputs of the strategic component. In those instances, we are interested in the return-on-investment (ROI). The ROI is simply a ratio of the increments in results brought about by the added resource investments.

```
┌─────────────────────────────────────────────────────────┐
│                                                         │
│      STAGE 3:  SELECTING PREFERRED COURSES OF ACTION    │
│                                                         │
└─────────────────────────────────────────────────────────┘
```

What Are Preferred Courses Of Action?

The preferred courses of action will be those that maximize the probability of achieving strategic goals while minimizing the costs.

How Are Courses Of Action Selected?

With the strategic goals for the organizational components identified, the next step is to make strategic decisions regarding alternative courses of action. The strategic decisions use the organizational values imbedded in the productivity mission to select the most cost beneficial courses of action.

Example

For example, in attempting to achieve a strategic personnel goal in the resource component, the consulting intervention may consider variations of the following basic strategies:

- **INCREASE CAPACITY:** Increase personnel by hiring.

- **ACQUIRE CAPACITY:** Purchase or subcontract personnel capacity.

- **DEVELOP CAPACITY:** Train existing personnel.

To choose among these alternative courses of action, the productivity values are used to make the most cost beneficial decisions. The preferred courses of action are those that will best satisfy the productivity values.

Summary

An instructional intervention is one of many courses of
action which may be selected. The preferred courses of
action should be those that maximize the probability of
achieving strategic goals. Therefore, if an instructional
intervention is selected, then the instructional designers
should understand the productivity values that entered into
the strategic decision-making process. These productivity
values should also be used to make decisions within the
instructional intervention.

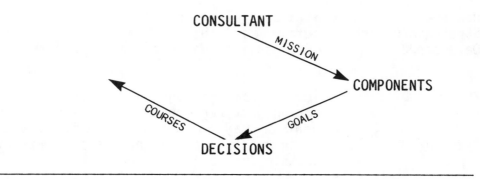

STAGE 4: DEVELOPING STRATEGIC PLANS

**What Are
Strategic Plans?**

Strategic plans are designs for implementing the preferred courses of action that enable the organization to achieve the strategic goals and productivity mission.

**How Are
Strategic Plans
Developed?**

Strategic plans are developed by identifying the tasks to be performed. The tasks define the responsibilities or duties of organizational units and performers.

Example

For example, having chosen a resource development course of action, strategic plans for making an instructional intervention may now be developed. The strategic plan for an instructional design intervention may include the following tasks:

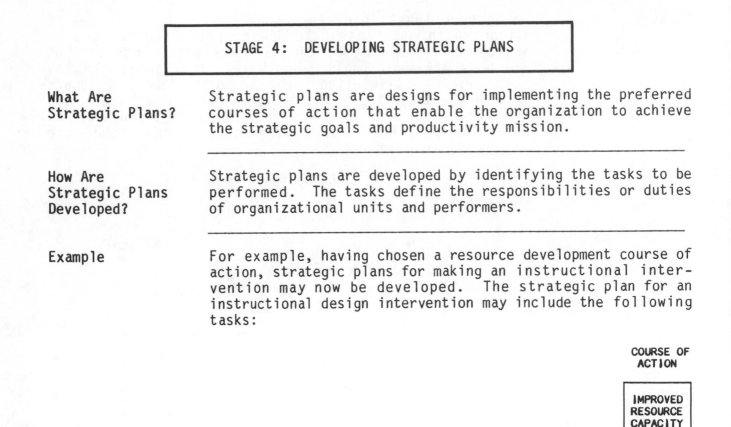

COURSE OF
ACTION

IMPROVED
RESOURCE
CAPACITY

Evaluate Goal
Achievement

Make Instructional
Intervention

Prepare Trainees to
Receive Instruction

Design Instructional
Delivery Plan

Develop Instructional
Content

Specify Instructional
Objectives

Analyze Contextual
Tasks

Refine Productivity
Goals

Receive Productivity
Mission/Goals

Summary

Strategic plans ensure that the selected courses of action
will be successfully implemented. Instructional design
personnel may participate in the design of strategic plans
when a personnel resource development course of action has
been selected. The remaining sections of this book describe
the instructional design tasks to be performed when training
is to be provided.

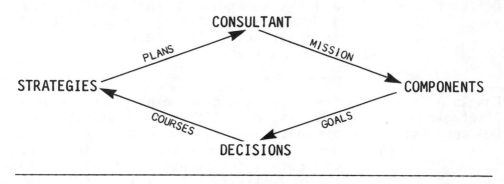

STAGE 5: MAKING THE STRATEGIC DELIVERY

What Is A Strategic Delivery?

A strategic delivery is the presentation of the strategic plans to decision makers. Most often, the decision makers are the managers of the various organizational components affected by the strategic plans. The strategic delivery is an opportunity for the decision makers to fine tune the strategic plans.

How Is A Strategic Delivery Made?

The strategic plans emphasizing organizational and individual responsibilities are presented to decision makers. The presentation may be made using any medium as long as decision makers are provided with an opportunity to process and refine the strategic plans. Decision makers may modify the productivity mission by changing the expected results in relation to the resource expenditures. Similarly, they may adjust the training resource expenditures in relation to the projected performance increments.

Summary

Strategic plans are not completed until a strategic delivery has been made. Decision makers process and refine the plans during the strategic delivery.

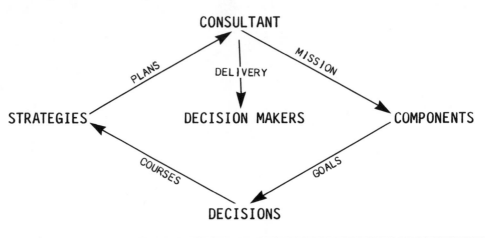

22

```
┌─────────────────────────────────────────────────┐
│  STAGE 6:  EVALUATING THE CONSULTING PROCESSES    │
└─────────────────────────────────────────────────┘
```

**What Is
Evaluating
The Strategic
Processes?**

Evaluation is the final stage in the strategic processes used during the consulting intervention. The results of the evaluation are used to refine the productivity mission, strategic goals, courses of action, and strategic plans.

**How Is The
Evaluation
Performed?**

The evaluation assesses all of the previous stages of the consulting intervention beginning with the strategic delivery stage. The following questions are asked:

STAGE	QUESTION
Making the Strategic Delivery	Are decision makers prepared to <u>receive</u> the presentation?
Developing Strategic Plans	Can decision makers <u>acquire</u> a full understanding of the strategic plans?
Selecting Preferred Courses of Action	Can decision makers <u>apply</u> the plans to implement the preferred courses of action?
Developing Strategic Goals	Can decision makers <u>transfer</u> the preferred courses of action to the strategic goals of their organizational components?
Formulating The Productivity Mission	Can decision makers <u>achieve</u> the productivity mission as originally formulated?

**How Are The
Results Used?**

The net effect of the evaluation is to ensure that the original productivity mission formulated by the executive officers will be achieved. Evaluation results are used as follows:

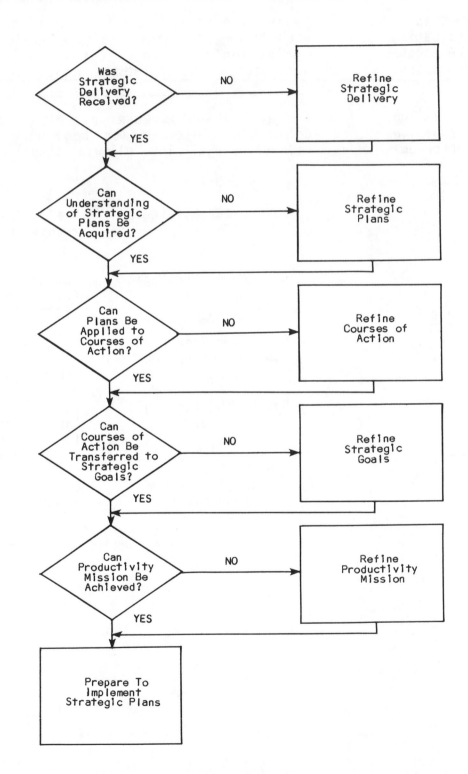

Summary

The evaluation of the consulting process can be thought of as a feedback loop. Policy makers initiate the consulting intervention. Key organizational decision makers (i.e., managers) process the results of the consulting intervention and provide feedback on the strategic plans, preferred courses of action, and strategic goals. Policy makers use this feedback to refine the original productivity mission.

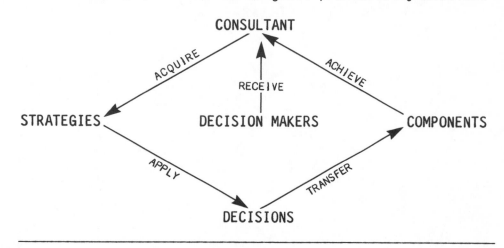

INSTRUCTIONAL
INTERVENTION
OVERVIEW

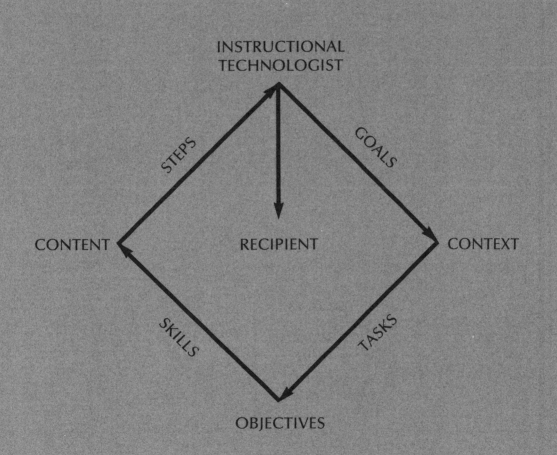

Introduction

We have all experienced an instructional intervention which was less successful than we had hoped. The trainees or recipients of our intervention participate fully in the training. The training receives good ratings from the recipients. However, when the recipients return to their work settings, they fail to use what we taught them.

Times are changing. The productivity age is upon us. We can no longer afford to design instructional interventions which do not yield changes in task performance and productivity.

Productive instructional interventions will only result from instructional designs that emphasize the systematic achievement of the productivity goals. This section presents a programmatic model for designing instructional interventions.

What Are The Components Of Instructional Design?

A programmatic instructional design has the following components:

- Instructional Technologist: The individual who designs, implements, and evaluates the instructional intervention.

- Recipient: The individual who is to receive the instructional intervention.

- Context: The tasks which must be performed by the recipient in the work setting.

- Objectives: The activities or outcomes which must be achieved by the recipient during the instructional intervention.

- Content: The skills, skill steps, and supportive knowledge to be delivered during the instructional intervention.

**How Is
Instruction
Designed?**

A programmatic instructional design includes the following activities:

1. Establishing Productivity Goals: Stating the desired results outputs and anticipated levels of resource inputs.

2. Analyzing Contextual Tasks: Identifying the tasks which must be performed in order to accomplish the desired productivity goals.

3. Specifying Training Objectives: Defining the components, functions, processes, conditions, and standards of the task performance to be acquired by recipients.

4. Developing Training Content: Detailing the skills, skill steps, and supportive knowledge which will lead to the achievement of the training objectives.

5. Planning Training Delivery: Determining the methods and media to be used for ensuring the effective delivery of the training content.

The following chapters describe each instructional design activity in detail.

ESTABLISHING PRODUCTIVITY GOALS

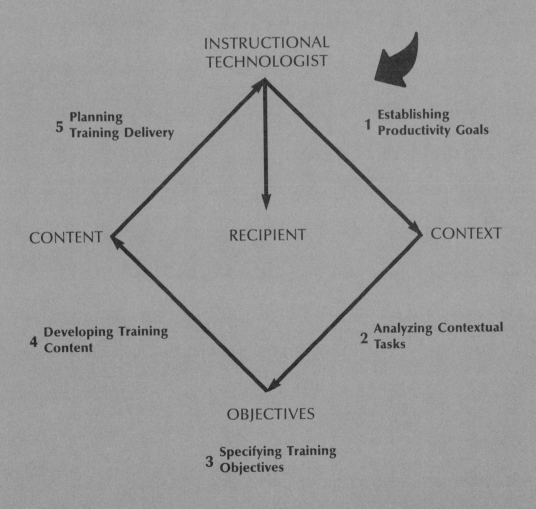

INSTRUCTIONAL
TECHNOLOGIST

5 Planning
Training Delivery

1 Establishing
Productivity Goals

CONTENT

RECIPIENT

CONTEXT

4 Developing Training
Content

2 Analyzing Contextual
Tasks

OBJECTIVES

3 Specifying Training
Objectives

> ### THE GOAL OF ALL INSTRUCTIONAL INTERVENTIONS
> ### IS AN IMPROVEMENT IN PRODUCTIVITY

**What Are
Productivity
Goals?**

During the consulting intervention, a productivity mission is formulated. Our first instructional design task is to establish refined productivity goals for the organizational units that will receive training. Productivity goals individualize the productivity mission to the units targeted for the intervention. The productivity goals are stated in terms of results outputs and/or resource inputs:

$$PRODUCTIVITY\ GOALS\ =\ \frac{RESULTS\ OUTPUTS\ (RO)}{RESOURCE\ INPUTS\ (RI)}$$

**Why
Productivity
Goals?**

A training intervention is meaningless unless we are trying to achieve some benefit for the organization and its employees. The methods used to achieve the desired results must be effective and efficient. By establishing a productivity goal, we can:

- Define the benefits we intend to achieve.

- Specify how much they will cost.

**When Are
Productivity
Goals Used?**

Productivity goals are used when planning and evaluating training interventions. Establishing a productivity goal sets the course to be followed during the training intervention. Once the training intervention has been made, then you can use the productivity goal to assess if the desired results were achieved using the anticipated amount of resources.

**How Are
Productivity
Goals Established?**

We establish refined productivity goals by completing the following steps:

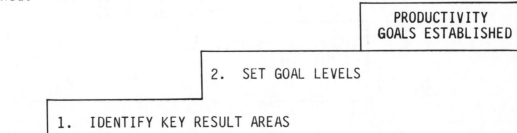

PRODUCTIVITY
GOALS ESTABLISHED

2. SET GOAL LEVELS

1. IDENTIFY KEY RESULT AREAS

STEP 1: IDENTIFY KEY RESULT AREAS

What Are Key Result Areas?

Key result areas are organizational outputs that are critical to the achievement of the productivity mission. Not all organizational outputs are key result areas. Rather, key result areas are the critical few outputs that account for most of the variance. Stated more simply, key result areas are the few results outputs that will make or break the organization.

KEY RESULT AREAS = CRITICAL FEW OUTPUTS

Why Are Key Result Areas Important?

The identification of key result areas allows us to focus our instructional resources on the critical organizational outputs. The potential Return-on-Investment is much greater since the resource inputs (e.g., training costs, personnel costs, etc.) are invested in the most highly valued results outputs. In other words, it is possible to get a larger return on each instructional dollar invested in maintaining or improving key result areas.

How Are Key Result Areas Identified?

The following substeps are used when identifying key result areas:

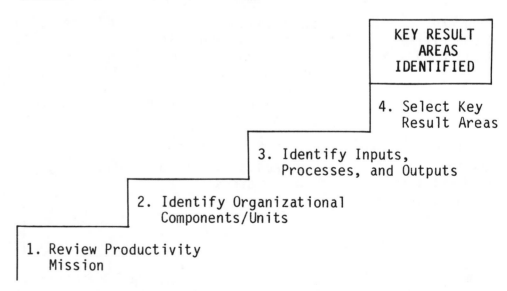

KEY RESULT AREAS IDENTIFIED

4. Select Key Result Areas

3. Identify Inputs, Processes, and Outputs

2. Identify Organizational Components/Units

1. Review Productivity Mission

Substep 1:
 Review
 Productivity
 Mission

The productivity mission is formulated during the consulting intervention. Most organizations have established a mission. As an instructional designer, your job is to review the mission in order to determine the target populations and organizational goals. If your organization has not formulated a mission, then you will need to work with policy makers or their representatives in order to identify target populations and organizational goals.

REMEMBER . . .

MISSION = ORGANIZATIONAL GOALS x TARGET POPULATIONS

Substep 2:
 Identify
 Organizational
 Components/
 Units

The next substep is to identify the organizational components/units within which your instructional intervention will take place. Following are examples of organizational components/units:

COMPONENTS	UNITS
RESOURCES	• Personnel Office • Comptroller's Office • Industrial Relations/ Training Division
PRODUCTION	• Engineering Division • Housing Program Area • Assembly Plant
MARKETING	• Advertising Office • Sales Division • Customer Complaints Division
DISTRIBUTION	• Public Relations Office • Shipping Divisions • Satellite Communications Center

Substep 3:
   Identify
   Inputs,
   Processes,
   and Outputs

You now know where the intervention will take place. The next substep is to identify the inputs, processes, and outputs for each organizational component/unit involved in the intervention.

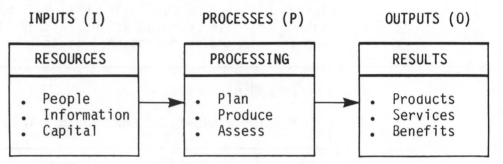

INPUTS (I)   PROCESSES (P)   OUTPUTS (O)

RESOURCES	PROCESSING	RESULTS
• People • Information • Capital	• Plan • Produce • Assess	• Products • Services • Benefits

<u>INPUTS:</u>   People, information, and/or capital resources which are used to accomplish the productivity mission.

<u>PROCESSES:</u> Inputs are processed by the organizational component/unit. Processing includes planning, producing, and assessing.

<u>OUTPUTS:</u>   Finished products, services, and/or benefits used to achieve the productivity mission.

Substep 4:
   Select Key
   Result Areas

The final substep is to select the key result areas from among the results outputs identified in the previous substep. The principle of the critical few should be used when selecting key result areas (i.e., outputs).

<u>RESOURCE COMPONENT</u>

PERSONNEL OFFICE
```
I → P → 0    ← Key Result
I → P → 0
I → P → 0
I → P → 0
```

TRAINING DIVISION
```
I → P → 0      Key Results
I → P → 0
I → P → 0
I → P → 0
```

┌───┐
│   STEP 2:   SET GOAL LEVELS   │
└───┘

What Is A Goal Level?

A goal level is simply the amount of desired change to occur in the results outputs and/or resource inputs for each key result area. The direction of the desired change in results outputs and/or resource inputs may be:

CHANGE	RESULTS OUTPUTS	RESOURCE INPUTS
Increase (+)		
Decrease (-)		
Maintain (0)		

Are There Ideal Goal Levels?

Ideally, goal levels should attempt to improve results outputs while reducing resource inputs. The ideal goal levels are as follows:

CHANGE	RESULTS OUTPUTS	RESOURCE INPUTS
Increase (+)	$+$ ✓	
Decrease (-)		$-$ ✓
Maintain (0)		

**What If The
Ideal Is Not
Possible?**

Most often, ideal goal levels are not possible. Frequently, it is necessary to increase the resource inputs in order to increase the results outputs. In these cases, goal levels are used to compare the increments in results with the resource expenditures. This comparison is called return-on-investment (ROI).

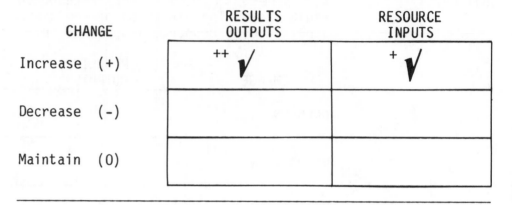

CHANGE	RESULTS OUTPUTS	RESOURCE INPUTS
Increase (+)	++ √	+ √
Decrease (−)		
Maintain (0)		

**Can The Resources
Ever Exceed
The Results?**

In very rare instances, goal levels may be set so that the resource inputs exceed the results outputs. This inverse of resources and results may be appropriate to resolve short-term performance crises. For example, sales continue to decline while a new product line is under development. A short-term intervention is needed to prevent further decline of the old product line while the development work is completed on the new product line.

CHANGE	RESULTS OUTPUTS	RESOURCE INPUTS
Increase (+)		+ √
Decrease (−)		
Maintain (0)	o √	

Why Are Goal Levels Set?

Goal levels tell us the amount of change to occur in each key result area included in our intervention. We also can get a before and after snapshot of the results outputs and resource inputs for all key result areas.

How Are Goal Levels Set?

The following substeps are used when setting goal levels for each key result area:

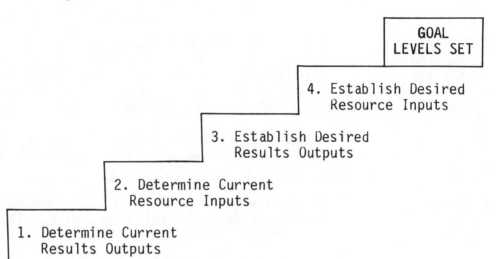

```
                                                    ┌─────────────┐
                                                    │    GOAL     │
                                                    │ LEVELS SET  │
                                                    └─────────────┘
                                          4. Establish Desired
                                             Resource Inputs
                              3. Establish Desired
                                 Results Outputs
                  2. Determine Current
                     Resource Inputs
      1. Determine Current
         Results Outputs
```

Substep 1: Determine Current Results Outputs

The first substep is to determine the current levels of results outputs for each key result area. Following are the quantitative measures and qualitative measures that can be used to assess the current results outputs:

QUANTITATIVE MEASURES	QUALITATIVE MEASURES
Volume: How many?	**Accuracy:** How well? Meet Standards?
Rate: How many per time unit?	**Functionality:** Does it work?
Timeliness: On time?	**Initiative:** Is it new?

NOTE: When possible, results output measures should be translated into dollar values.

Continued . . .

Substep 1:
(Continued)

Combined quantitative/qualitative measures may be used to measure results outputs. The following example includes both a measure of rate and a measure of accuracy:

Rate ➡ ⟮ Analysts review five financial statements per week ⟯

                                                                    Accuracy

⟮ while detecting 50% of all diversions of funds. ⟯ ➴

Substep 2:
Determine
Current
Resource
Inputs

A list of resource inputs was generated while identifying key result areas (see previous step). We now identify the resource inputs that are directly and indirectly associated with the key result areas. Finally, an actual or approximate dollar value is attached to each resource input.

Remember, there are personnel, information, and capital resources associated with most key result areas.

Example

The following example illustrates how resource inputs may be determined for a training area within the resource component of an organization.

KEY RESULT AREA: Train supervisory personnel to improve on-the-job performance.

RESOURCE INPUTS PER TRAINING DAY:

PERSONNEL
- Training Staff $ 50/Trainee
  (@ 1 trainer per 10 trainees)
- Trainee's Time $600/Trainee
  (average salary + fringe + G&A)
- Loss of Production While $500/Trainee
  in Training*

INFORMATION
- Training Materials* $ 25/Trainee

CAPITAL
- Space and Energy* $ 10/Trainee
- Audio and Visual Equipment* $ 5/Trainee

*Based on historical data

APPROXIMATE RESOURCE INPUTS:

$1,190 per trainee for each training day

Substep 3:
  Establish
  Desired
  Results Outputs

Once we have a picture of the current level of results outputs, then we establish desired levels of results outputs. To establish the desired level of results outputs we:

ESTABLISH DESIRED LEVEL OF RESULTS OUTPUTS

1	Determine the direction (i.e., increase, decrease, or maintain) and the amount of change desired for each results output.
2	Decide if quantitative and/or qualitative measures will be used to measure the amount of change.
3	Select the most appropriate method and unit of measurement. **METHODS OF MEASUREMENT** . Volume . Accuracy . Rate . Functionality . Timeliness . Initiative **UNITS OF MEASUREMENT** . # of _____ . # of _____ per _____ . As measured by _____
4	. Establish a numerical or descriptive value for all results outputs. . If possible, translate the results outputs to dollar values.

Example

Table 3 provides an example of quantitative and qualitative measures of results outputs.

41

Table 3.

QUANTITATIVE AND QUALITATIVE MEASURES OF RESULTS OUTPUTS

	METHOD	EXAMPLES
QUANTITATIVE MEASURES	Volume: How many? Rate: How many per time unit? Timeliness: On time?	• Engineers will produce 3 alternative designs on all projects. • Typists will increase their output to a minimum of 10 pages per hour. • Auditors will complete all review of financial statements within two weeks of receipt.
QUALITATIVE MEASURES	Accuracy: How well? Meet standards? Functionality: Does it work? Initiative: Is it new?	• Typists will have no more than 4 typos per 10 pages. • Managers will be rated a minimum of a level 3 on a 5-point management skills rating scale. • ADP systems analysts will design a management information system rated as useful to personnel decision makers. • Information specialists will develop a new method for using data to generate future scenarios.

NOTE: Remember, quantitative and qualitative measures may be applied to a single results output. Also, when possible, these measures should be converted to a dollar value.

Substep 4:
Establish
Desired
Resource
Inputs

The current and desired results outputs have been established. We also know the cost of the current resource inputs. The final piece of the goal equation is to establish the desired level of resource inputs. The amount of resource inputs to be expended should be related to the amount of results outputs to be achieved.

ESTABLISH DESIRED LEVEL OF RESOURCE INPUTS	
1	Determine the direction (i.e., increase, decrease, or maintain) and the amount of change desired for each resource input.
2	Establish a dollar value for anticipated resource inputs, including: • Personnel • Information • Capital

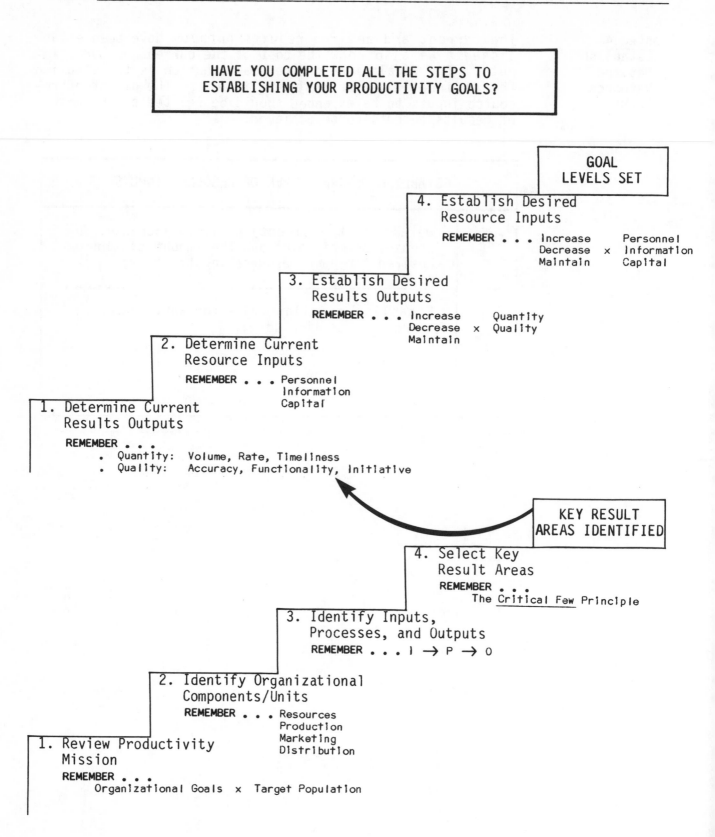

HAVE YOU COMPLETED ALL THE STEPS TO
ESTABLISHING YOUR PRODUCTIVITY GOALS?

GOAL
LEVELS SET

4. Establish Desired
Resource Inputs

REMEMBER . . . Increase   Personnel
Decrease x Information
Maintain   Capital

3. Establish Desired
Results Outputs

REMEMBER . . . Increase   Quantity
Decrease x Quality
Maintain

2. Determine Current
Resource Inputs

REMEMBER . . . Personnel
Information
Capital

1. Determine Current
Results Outputs

REMEMBER . . .
. Quantity: Volume, Rate, Timeliness
. Quality: Accuracy, Functionality, Initiative

KEY RESULT
AREAS IDENTIFIED

4. Select Key
Result Areas
REMEMBER . . .
The Critical Few Principle

3. Identify Inputs,
Processes, and Outputs
REMEMBER . . . I → P → O

2. Identify Organizational
Components/Units

REMEMBER . . . Resources
Production
Marketing
Distribution

1. Review Productivity
Mission
REMEMBER . . .
Organizational Goals x Target Population

ESTABLISHING PRODUCTIVITY GOALS

Job Aids

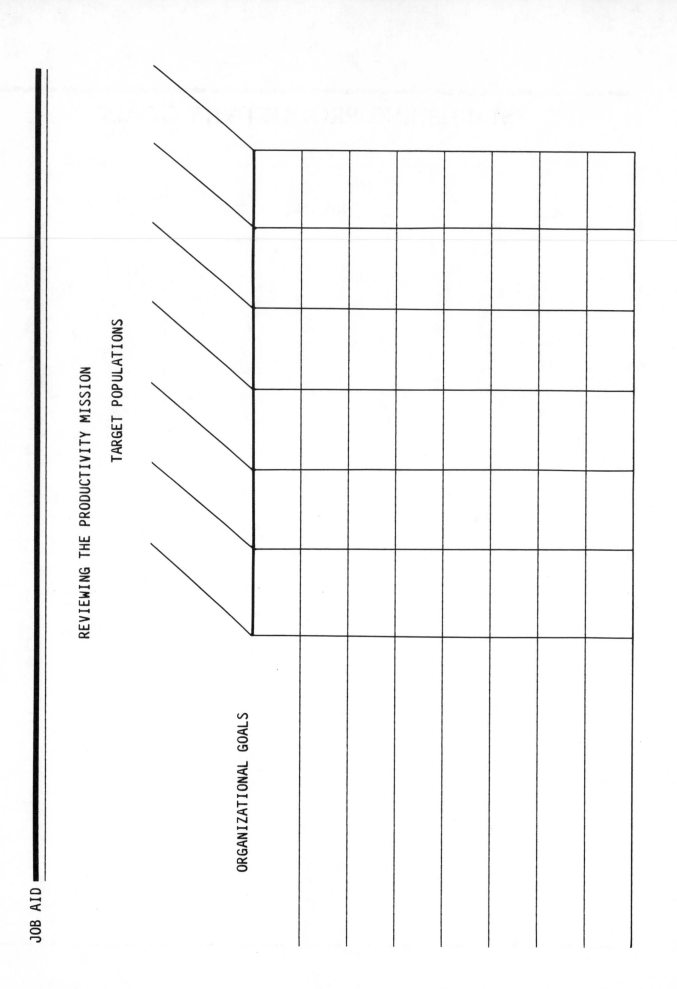

JOB AID

REVIEWING THE PRODUCTIVITY MISSION

TARGET POPULATIONS

ORGANIZATIONAL GOALS

SAMPLE

REVIEWING THE PRODUCTIVITY MISSION

TARGET POPULATIONS

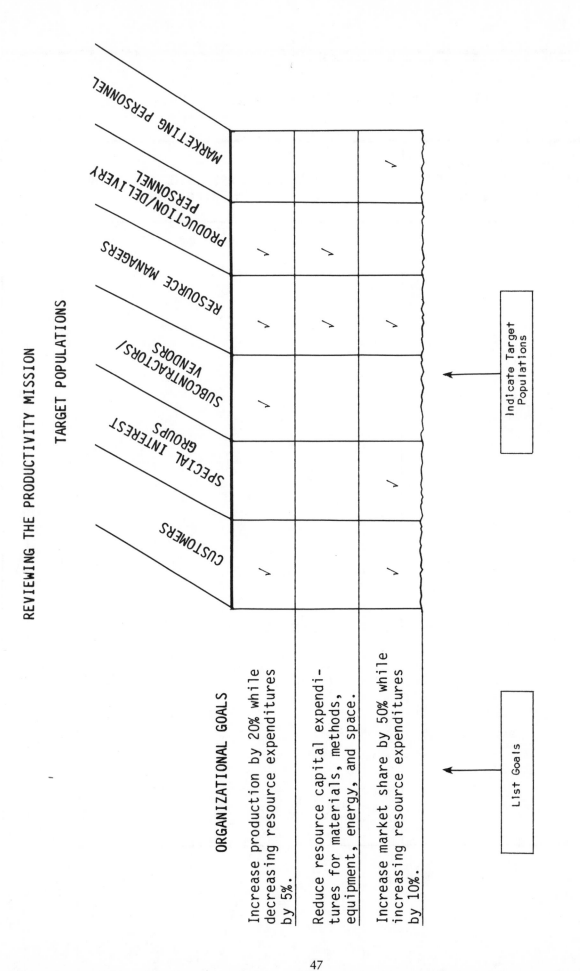

ORGANIZATIONAL GOALS	CUSTOMERS	SPECIAL INTEREST GROUPS	SUBCONTRACTORS/ VENDORS	RESOURCE MANAGERS	PRODUCTION/DELIVERY PERSONNEL	MARKETING PERSONNEL
Increase production by 20% while decreasing resource expenditures by 5%.	✓		✓	✓	✓	
Reduce resource capital expenditures for materials, methods, equipment, energy, and space.				✓	✓	
Increase market share by 50% while increasing resource expenditures by 10%.	✓	✓		✓		✓

Indicate Target Populations

List Goals

47

IDENTIFYING ORGANIZATIONAL COMPONENTS/UNITS

WHAT ORGANIZATIONAL COMPONENTS ARE INVOLVED IN THE INTERVENTION?	WHAT UNITS ARE INVOLVED IN THE INTERVENTION?

IDENTIFYING ORGANIZATIONAL COMPONENTS/UNITS

WHAT ORGANIZATIONAL COMPONENTS ARE INVOLVED IN THE INTERVENTION?	WHAT UNITS ARE INVOLVED IN THE INTERVENTION?

RESOURCES	• Personnel Office
	
	    • Recruitment Staff
	    • Training Staff
	    • EEO Staff

PRODUCTION	• First- and third-shift assembly line

Identify
Organizational
Components

Specify the Units Within
The Organizational
Components

JOB AID

- IDENTIFYING INPUTS, PROCESSES, AND OUTPUTS
- SELECTING KEY RESULT AREAS

ORGANIZATIONAL COMPONENTS/ AREAS	INPUTS	PROCESSES	OUTPUTS	KEY RESULTS ✓

SAMPLE

- IDENTIFYING INPUTS, PROCESSES, AND OUTPUTS
- SELECTING KEY RESULT AREAS

ORGANIZATIONAL COMPONENTS/ AREAS	INPUTS	PROCESSES	OUTPUTS	√ KEY RESULTS
RESOURCE COMPONENT Training Office	Personnel: • Trainers • Trainees' time Information: • Training materials • Training needs assessment Capital: • Audio and visual equipment • Space and energy	Plan: • Establish productivity goal • Analyze contextual tasks • Specify training objectives • Develop the skills content • Develop training delivery and evaluation plan Produce: • Develop training materials • Deliver content to trainees Assess: • Evaluate process, acquisition, application, transfer, and productivity • Transmit results and new training technologies	Products: • Training curricula • Self-instructional materials • Improved training technologies Services: • Technical assistance program • Follow-up services Benefits: • Skilled personnel • Improved task performance on the job for supervisory personnel	 √ √

Indicate Areas Where Intervention Will Occur →

Specify Resource Inputs →

List the Processes →

Determine Resource Outputs →

Select Those Outputs That Are Key Result Areas →

51

DETERMINING CURRENT RESULTS OUTPUTS

KEY RESULT AREA:

TYPE OF MEASUREMENT	METHOD OF MEASUREMENT	SPECIFY CURRENT LEVEL OF RESULTS OUTPUTS
QUANTITATIVE	☐ VOLUME ☐ RATE ☐ TIMELINESS ☐ QUANTITY NOT APPLICABLE	
QUALITATIVE	☐ ACCURACY ☐ FUNCTIONALITY ☐ INITIATIVE ☐ QUALITY NOT APPLICABLE	
COMBINED QUANTITATIVE/ QUALITATIVE	☐ VOLUME ☐ RATE ☐ TIMELINESS ☐ ACCURACY ☐ FUNCTIONALITY ☐ INITIATIVE ☐ NOT APPLICABLE	

DETERMINING CURRENT RESULTS OUTPUTS

KEY RESULT AREA:

Train supervisory personnel to improve on-the-job performance.

TYPE OF MEASUREMENT	METHOD OF MEASUREMENT	SPECIFY CURRENT LEVEL OF RESULTS OUTPUTS
QUANTITATIVE	☑ VOLUME ☐ RATE ☐ TIMELINESS ☐ QUANTITY NOT APPLICABLE	300 supervisors receive training each year.
QUALITATIVE	☑ ACCURACY ☐ FUNCTIONALITY ☐ INITIATIVE ☐ QUALITY NOT APPLICABLE	On the average, supervisors' skills are rated 1.5 on a 5-point supervisory skills rating scale when they return to the work setting after training.

Specify the Current Performance Level

Indicate the Method(s) of Measurement

Specify the Key Result Area

DETERMINING CURRENT RESOURCE INPUTS

KEY RESULT AREA:

RESOURCE CATEGORY	ITEMIZE		TOTAL DOLLAR VALUE
	ITEMS	$	
PERSONNEL			
	ITEMS	$	
INFORMATION			
	ITEMS	$	
CAPITAL			

TOTAL COST OF CURRENT RESOURCE INPUTS:

DETERMINING CURRENT RESOURCE INPUTS

KEY RESULT AREA:

Train supervisory personnel to improve on-the-job performance.

RESOURCE CATEGORY	ITEMS	ITEMIZE	TOTAL DOLLAR VALUE
PERSONNEL	• Training staff • Trainee's time • Loss of production	$ $ 50/trainee x 3 days $600/trainee x 3 days $500/trainee x 3 days	$3,450/trainee
INFORMATION	• Training materials	$ $ 25/trainee x 3 days	$ 75/trainee
CAPITAL	• Space and energy	$ $ 10/trainee x 3 days $ 5/trainee x 3 days	$ 45/trainee

Specify the Key Result Area

Determine the Dollar Amount of Each Resource Item

Total Each Category

ESTABLISHING DESIRED RESULTS OUTPUTS

KEY RESULT AREA:

TYPE OF MEASUREMENT	DIRECTION OF CHANGE	METHOD OF MEASUREMENT	SPECIFY DESIRED LEVEL OF RESULTS OUTPUTS
QUANTITATIVE	☐ INCREASE ☐ DECREASE ☐ MAINTAIN	☐ VOLUME ☐ RATE ☐ TIMELINESS ☐ QUANTITY NOT APPLICABLE	
QUALITATIVE	☐ INCREASE ☐ DECREASE ☐ MAINTAIN	☐ ACCURACY ☐ FUNCTIONALITY ☐ INITIATIVE ☐ QUALITY NOT APPLICABLE	
COMBINED QUANTITATIVE/ QUALITATIVE	☐ INCREASE ☐ DECREASE ☐ MAINTAIN	☐ VOLUME ☐ RATE ☐ TIMELINESS ☐ ACCURACY ☐ FUNCTIONALITY ☐ INITIATIVE ☐ NOT APPLICABLE	

56

ESTABLISHING DESIRED RESULTS OUTPUTS

KEY RESULT AREA:

Train supervisory personnel to improve on-the-job performance.

TYPE OF MEASUREMENT	DIRECTION OF CHANGE	METHOD OF MEASUREMENT	SPECIFY DESIRED LEVEL OF RESULTS OUTPUTS
QUANTITATIVE	☐ INCREASE ☐ DECREASE ☑ MAINTAIN	☑ VOLUME ☐ RATE ☐ TIMELINESS ☐ QUANTITY NOT APPLICABLE	300 supervisors will receive training each year.
QUALITATIVE	☑ INCREASE ☐ DECREASE ☐ MAINTAIN	☑ ACCURACY ☐ FUNCTIONALITY ☐ INITIATIVE ☐ QUALITY NOT APPLICABLE	On the average, supervisors will be rated 3.0 on a 5-point supervisory skills rating scale when they return to the work setting after training.

Specify the Key Result Area

Indicate the Direction of the Change Desired

Select the Method of Measurement To Be Used

Specify the Desired Performance Level To Be Achieved

JOB AID

ESTABLISHING DESIRED RESOURCE INPUTS

KEY RESULT AREA:

RESOURCE CATEGORY	DIRECTION OF CHANGE	ITEMIZE	
		ITEMS	TOTAL DOLLAR VALUE
PERSONNEL	☐ INCREASE ☐ DECREASE ☐ MAINTAIN	ITEMS	$
INFORMATION	☐ INCREASE ☐ DECREASE ☐ MAINTAIN	ITEMS	$
CAPITAL	☐ INCREASE ☐ DECREASE ☐ MAINTAIN	ITEMS	$
			TOTAL COST OF ANTICIPATED RESOURCE INPUTS

ESTABLISHING DESIRED RESOURCE INPUTS

KEY RESULTS AREA:

Train supervisory personnel to improve on-the-job performance.

RESOURCE CATEGORY	DIRECTION OF CHANGE	ITEMIZE		TOTAL DOLLAR VALUE
		ITEMS	$	
PERSONNEL	☐ INCREASE ☑ DECREASE ☐ MAINTAIN	• Training staff • Trainee's time • Loss of production	$ 50/trainee x 2.5 days $600/trainee x 2.5 days $500/trainee x 2.5 days	$2,875/trainee
		ITEMS	$	
INFORMATION	☐ INCREASE ☑ DECREASE ☐ MAINTAIN	• Training materials	$ 25/trainee x 2.5 days	$62.50/trainee
		ITEMS	$	
CAPITAL	☐ INCREASE ☑ DECREASE ☐ MAINTAIN	• Space and energy • Audio-and-visual equipment	$ 10/trainee x 2.5 days $ 5/trainee x 2.5 days	$37.50/trainee

Total Each Category

Specify the Dollar Amount of All Anticipated Resource Expenditures

Indicate the Direction of the Change Desired

Specify the Key Result Area

ANALYZING CONTEXTUAL TASKS

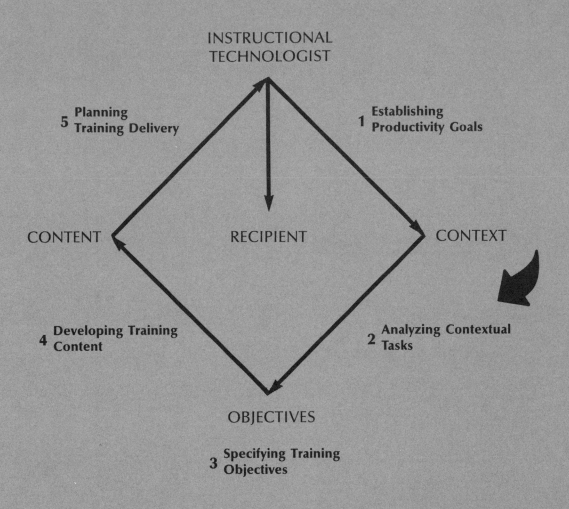

INSTRUCTIONAL
TECHNOLOGIST

5 Planning
Training Delivery

1 Establishing
Productivity Goals

CONTENT

RECIPIENT

CONTEXT

4 Developing Training
Content

2 Analyzing Contextual
Tasks

OBJECTIVES

3 Specifying Training
Objectives

THE PURSUIT OF A PRODUCTIVITY GOAL REQUIRES
AN ANALYSIS OF THE CONTEXTUAL TASKS

What Is An Analysis Of Contextual Tasks?

By establishing a productivity goal, we have defined our desired results outputs and resource inputs. A contextual analysis simply:

- Identifies the tasks which must be performed to accomplish the productivity goals.

- Assesses barriers to task performance by delivery, supervisory, and managerial personnel.

Why Conduct An Analysis Of Contextual Tasks?

We analyze contextual tasks in order to understand what types of interventions are needed. Based on the results of the contextual analysis, training and nontraining objectives can be selected for the intervention. A training objective derived from an analysis of contextual tasks will be directly linked to that work environment. An impact on work performance (i.e., achievement of a productivity goal) can only result from interventions which are directly linked to the work setting. An analysis of contextual tasks serves as the link between the intervention objectives and the productivity goal.

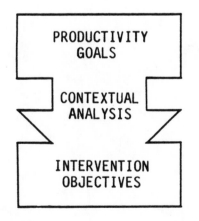

PRODUCTIVITY
GOALS

CONTEXTUAL
ANALYSIS

INTERVENTION
OBJECTIVES

When Is A Contextual Analysis Conducted?

A contextual analysis is conducted after productivity goals have been established and before training objectives are set.

How Are Contextual Tasks Analyzed?

We analyze contextual tasks by completing the following steps:

```
                                          ┌─────────────────┐
                                          │   CONTEXTUAL    │
                                          │ TASKS ANALYZED  │
                              ┌───────────┴─────────────────┘
                              │ 2. ASSESS CONTEXTUAL
                              │    BARRIERS
                  ┌───────────┘
                  │ 1. IDENTIFY PROCESS
                  │    TASKS
                  │
```

STEP 1: IDENTIFY PROCESS TASKS

**What Are
Process Tasks?**

Process tasks are the groups of work activities that must be performed to achieve the productivity goals. Delivery, supervisory, and management personnel perform process tasks.

**Why Are
Process Tasks
Important?**

In the previous section we focused on the resource inputs and results outputs. The process tasks are the means by which resource inputs are converted to results outputs.

RESOURCE INPUTS ⟶ PROCESSES ⟶ RESULTS OUTPUTS

Tasks ⟋

Productivity goals $\left(\dfrac{\text{RESULTS OUTPUTS}}{\text{RESOURCE INPUTS}} \right)$ can only be achieved through the performance of process tasks.

**How Are
Process Tasks
Identified?**

The general processes of each key result area were identified in Step 1 of Establishing Productivity Goals. Now, we can specify the tasks to be performed by delivery, supervisory, and managerial personnel within these general processes. The following substeps may be completed when identifying process tasks:

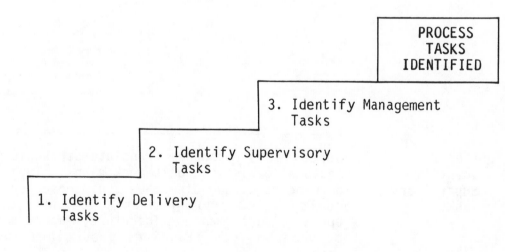

PROCESS
TASKS
IDENTIFIED

3. Identify Management
   Tasks

2. Identify Supervisory
   Tasks

1. Identify Delivery
   Tasks

What Techniques Are Available For Collecting Task Data?

The most common techniques used for collecting data about process tasks are:

- Observation
- Questionnaires
- Interviews
- Diary/Log
- Panel of Experts

Table 4 summarizes information about the various collection techniques.

Substep 1: Identify Delivery Tasks

Delivery personnel translate resource inputs into the desired results outputs. Delivery personnel include all types of workers such as assembly line workers, construction crews, scientists, accountants, computer programmers, and instructional designers.

To identify delivery tasks, we analyze the planning, producing, and assessing processes performed by delivery personnel in each key result area.

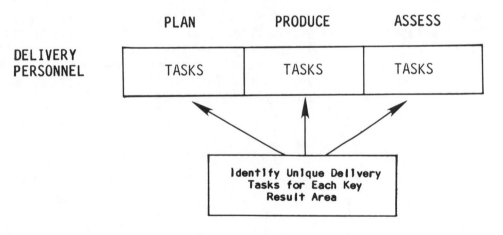

Substep 2: Identify Supervisory Tasks

Supervisory personnel translate strategic plans and organizational goals into unit work plans. Typically, supervisors develop tasks and directions, diagnose performance, set unit goals, develop programmatic methods, control work, and appraise performance. Therefore, supervisory tasks can also be grouped into planning, producing, and assessing processes.

Continued . . .

Table 4.

COLLECTING DATA ON PROCESS TASKS

TECHNIQUE . . .	OPTIONS . . .	USE WHEN . . .

OBSERVATION	• Direct
	• Videotape
	• Voice Recording
		• Jobs being analyzed have:
		  - Short duration cycles
		  - Observable work cycles.
		• Workers are unable to verbally describe their job tasks.
		• Trained observers are available.

INTERVIEWS	• Individual • Group	• Job tasks cannot be derived through observation. • Verification of facts collected through other methods, such as observation or written questionnaires, is required.
QUESTIONNAIRES	• Open-Ended • Closed or Fixed Responses	• Jobs being analyzed include white-collar, professional, managerial, or administrative personnel. • Cost is a primary value. • Validation of facts collected through other methods is required.
DIARY/LOG	• Self-Reporting Diary • Self-Reporting Time/Activity Log	• Collecting baseline information on tasks performed and percentage of time spent on each task is required. • Workers have made a commitment to collecting job performance data.
PANEL OF EXPERTS	• In-House Experts • External Experts	• Jobs are in transition or newly created. • Structuring questionnaire or other data collection instruments.

NOTE: Almost any combination of the above-described techniques will achieve
better results than a single technique used alone.

Substep 2:
  (Continued)

Supervisory tasks, unlike delivery tasks, are generic. Tasks performed in one key result area are similar to those supervisory tasks performed in all other key result areas. During this substep we individualize the generic supervisory tasks to each key result area.

	PLAN	PRODUCE	ASSESS
SUPERVISORY PERSONNEL	TASKS	TASKS	TASKS
DELIVERY PERSONNEL	TASKS	TASKS	TASKS

Individualize Supervisory Tasks For Each Key Result Area

Substep 3:
  Identify
  Management
  Tasks

Management personnel translate the mission into strategic plans and organizational goals. Typically, managers develop strategic plans, plan and acquire resource inputs, provide direction to supervisory personnel, and assess goal/mission fulfillment.

Management tasks also fall into the general categories of processes: planning, producing, and assessing. In addition, management tasks are similar to supervisory tasks in that they are generic. Our job is to individualize the generic management tasks to each key result area.

	PLAN	PRODUCE	ASSESS
MANAGEMENT PERSONNEL	TASKS	TASKS	TASKS
SUPERVISORY PERSONNEL	TASKS	TASKS	TASKS
DELIVERY PERSONNEL	TASKS	TASKS	TASKS

Individualize Management Tasks For Each Key Result Area

Example

Table 5 on the following page presents examples of the types of process tasks that may be performed by delivery, supervisory, and management personnel.

Table 5.

TYPES OF PROCESS TASKS

	PLAN	PRODUCE	ASSESS
MANAGEMENT	• Develop Goals • Make Strategic Decisions • Select Preferred Courses of Action • Develop Strategic Plans/Priorities • Plan Resource Acquisition	• Acquire Resources • Implement Strategic Plans • Provide Direction to Supervisory Personnel	• Track Results Outputs • Monitor Expenditure of Resource Inputs • Assess Goal and Mission Achievement • Appraise Supervisory Performance
SUPERVISORY	• Develop Work Unit Goals • Develop Task Assignments • Organize Work Assignments/Resources • Diagnose Performance	• Coordinate Resources • Direct Work • Develop Programmatic Methods/Procedures • Control Work/Resource Expenditures	• Track Results Outputs • Monitor Expenditure of Resource Inputs • Assess Results Outputs • Assess Resource Inputs • Appraise Employee Performance
DELIVERY	• Gather and Assemble Materials • Schedule Activities • Develop Individual Work Plans	• Perform Specific Job Tasks • Transmit Products	• Check Results Outputs • Document Use of Resource Inputs

---

STEP 2:   ASSESS CONTEXTUAL BARRIERS

**What Are
Contextual
Barriers?**

Contextual barriers are any source which prevents the performance of the process tasks. The three primary sources of contextual barriers are the personnel, the environment or organization, and information. There are physical, emotional, and intellectual dimensions to each of these sources.

BARRIER DIMENSIONS

BARRIER SOURCES	PHYSICAL	EMOTIONAL	INTELLECTUAL
PERSONNEL	Capacity?	Motives?	Skills?
ENVIRONMENT	Resources?	Incentives?	Procedures?
INFORMATION	Tasks?	Mission?	Flow?

**Why Are
Contextual
Barriers
Assessed?**

We assess contextual barriers in order to identify obstacles to task performance. Contextual barriers can be addressed through an instructional intervention or an additional consulting intervention.

USE . . .	WHEN . . .
Instructional Intervention	Primary Barrier is Personnel's Skills/Knowledge
Consulting Intervention	Primary Barriers are Outside Personnel's Skills/Knowledge

The instructional intervention removes barriers created by unskilled delivery, supervisory, or management personnel. The consulting intervention removes barriers by changing the organization. The consulting intervention yields strategic plans and enabling tasks. Enabling tasks are those tasks necessary to support the process tasks.

Example:
Process Tasks
vs.
Enabling Tasks

The following example illustrates the difference between a process task and an enabling task.

PROCESS TASK: To establish and maintain an accurate data base.

ENABLING TASKS: . To provide sufficient computer and programming resources.
. To provide timely flow of data.
. To offer incentives for initiative work on the data base.

Most often enabling tasks are performed by supervisory or managerial personnel. When enabling tasks are not being performed, then a barrier analysis can be used to determine if an instructional intervention is required at the supervisory or managerial levels.

REMEMBER . . .

What appears to be a nontraining barrier at one level within an organizational structure may be a skills/knowledge barrier at the next level up in the organization.

How Are Contextual Barriers Assessed?

The following substeps are completed when assessing contextual barriers:

CONTEXTUAL
BARRIERS
IDENTIFIED

2. Continue Barrier Analysis (if needed)

1. Identify Delivery-Level Barriers

What Techniques Are Available For Collecting Barrier Data?

The most common techniques used for collecting data about contextual barriers are to interview or survey job incumbents and their supervisors. In some cases, work measurement studies of task performance may be conducted. More formal research methods should only be used when rigorous data are needed. Often, opinion data are acceptable for the analysis of contextual barriers.

Substep 1:
Identify
Delivery-Level
Barriers

We begin our assessment by identifying barriers to task performance at the delivery level. A list of typical symptoms to look for during the barrier analysis is presented in Table 6 on the following page.

> **NOTE:** On occasion, the instructional designer may be asked to intervene at only one level within the organization. When this is the case, the instructional designer should conduct the barrier analysis at the organizational level of the selected target population. For example, the instructional designer may be asked to provide supervisory skills training. In this case, we may only want to assess barriers at the supervisory level of the organization.

Table 6.

CHECKING FOR CONTEXTUAL BARRIERS

	PHYSICAL	EMOTIONAL	INTELLECTUAL

P E R S O N N E L	CAPACITY
	✓ Lack of Strength
	✓ Lack of Dexterity
	✓ Lack of Stamina
	✓ Lack of Attentive-
	  ness
	✓ Lack of Concentration
	✓ Inability to Learn
	  New Tasks
		MOTIVES
		✓ Lack of Internalized
		  Reward System
		✓ Lack of Personalized
		  Goals
		✓ Lack of Initiative
		✓ Personnel Values
		  Inconsistent with
		  Mission
			SKILLS/KNOWLEDGE
			✓ Lack of Basic Skills
			✓ Lack of Specific
			  Task-Related Skill
			✓ Inadequate Knowledge
			  of Procedures and
			  Policies
			✓ Inadequate Under-
			  standing of Sup-
			  portive Knowledge

E N V I R O N M E N T	RESOURCES
	✓ Inadequate Personnel
	✓ Inadequate Raw
	  Materials
	✓ Inadequate Supplies
	✓ Inadequate Equipment
	✓ Inadequate Space
	✓ Inadequate Support
	  Services
	✓ Inadequate Energy
		INCENTIVES
		✓ Good Performance Is
		  Not Positively
		  Reinforced
		✓ Poor Performance Is
		  Positively Rein-
		  forced
		✓ Poor Performance Is
		  Not Linked to
		  Negative Conse-
		  quences
			PROCEDURES/METHODS
			✓ Out-of-Date Methods
			✓ Unreasonable
			  Deadlines
			✓ Unclear Chain of
			  Command
			✓ Unclear Reporting
			  Structure
			✓ Lack of Access to
			  Decision Process
			✓ Work Not Oriented
			  to Performers
			✓ Extensive Paperwork/
			  Red Tape

I N F O R M A T I O N	TASK EXPECTATIONS
	✓ Inconsistent Task
	  Requirements
	✓ Conflicting Time
	  Demands
	✓ Inadequate Task
	  Assignment
	✓ Unnecessarily Complex
	  Tasks
	✓ Boring, Repetitive
	  Tasks
	✓ Duplicative Task
	  Assignments
	✓ Infrequently Used
	  Tasks
		MISSION
		✓ No Policy
		✓ Conflicting Policies
		✓ Changing Policies
		✓ Conflicting Assign-
		  ment
		✓ Organizational Goals
		  Inconsistent With
		  Mission
			INFORMATION FLOW
			✓ Changing Information
			✓ Lack of Information
			✓ Lack of Accurate
			  Data
			✓ Lack of Timely Data
			✓ Lack of Complete
			  Data
			✓ Lack of Feedback
			✓ Lack of Monitoring

NOTE: These checks can be used when assessing contextual barriers at any
         level within the organization.

Substep 2:
  Continue
  Barrier
  Analysis
  (If Needed)

Further analysis of barriers at the supervisory and/or management levels may be needed when the assessment of delivery-level barriers finds obstacles in any of the following cells:

	PHYSICAL	EMOTIONAL	INTELLECTUAL
PERSONNEL	Capacity	Motives	Skills/ Knowledge
ENVIRONMENT	Resources √	Incentives √	Procedures √
INFORMATION	Task Expectations √	Mission	Flow √

If further analysis is warranted, simply recycle the process used when assessing the delivery-level barriers. Begin with the supervisory level. The results of this assessment will help you determine if the analysis should be applied to the management level.

What Are The
Outcomes Of A
Barrier Analysis?

The analysis of contextual barriers may point out the need for:

• An Instructional Intervention

• An Analysis of Recruitment and Selection Procedures and Policies

• Job Redesign

• An Additional Consulting Intervention so that Enabling Tasks can be Identified

Table 7 on the following page summarizes the possible outcomes of the barrier analysis.

74

Table 7.

POSSIBLE OUTCOMES OF THE BARRIER ANALYSIS

	PHYSICAL	EMOTIONAL	INTELLECTUAL
P E R S O N N E L	CAPACITY • Analyze Recruitment and Selection • Consider Job Redesign • Consider Physical Conditioning Training	MOTIVES • Analyze Recruitment and Selection • Consider Job Redesign • Review Incentives	SKILLS/KNOWLEDGE • Provide Training to Delivery Personnel • Develop Job Aids
E N V I R O N M E N T	RESOURCES • Conduct Barrier Analysis on Supervisory and/or Managerial Tasks - OR - • Recommend That a Consulting Intervention be Conducted	INCENTIVES • Conduct Barrier Analysis on Supervisory and/or Managerial Tasks - OR - • Recommend That a Consulting Intervention be Conducted	PROCEDURES/METHODS • Conduct Barrier Analysis on Supervisory and/or Managerial Tasks - OR - • Recommend That a Consulting Intervention be Conducted
I N F O R M A T I O N	TASK EXPECTATIONS • Conduct Barrier Analysis on Supervisory and/or Managerial Tasks - OR - • Recommend That a Consulting Intervention be Conducted	MISSION • Recommend That a Consulting Intervention be Conducted	INFORMATION FLOW • Conduct Barrier Analysis on Supervisory and/or Managerial Tasks - OR - • Recommend That a Consulting Intervention be Conducted

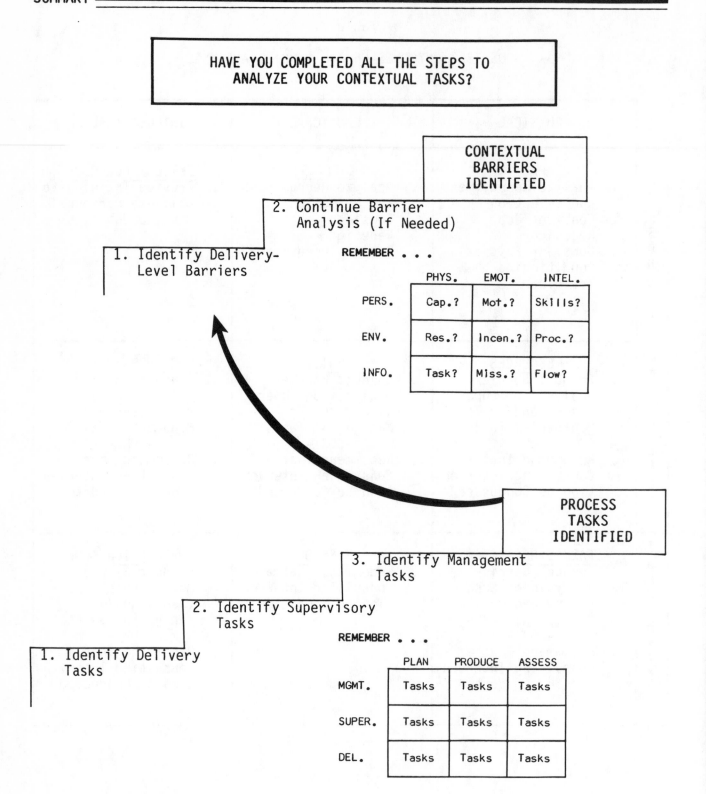

HAVE YOU COMPLETED ALL THE STEPS TO
ANALYZE YOUR CONTEXTUAL TASKS?

CONTEXTUAL
BARRIERS
IDENTIFIED

2. Continue Barrier
Analysis (If Needed)

1. Identify Delivery-
Level Barriers

REMEMBER . . .

	PHYS.	EMOT.	INTEL.
PERS.	Cap.?	Mot.?	Skills?
ENV.	Res.?	Incen.?	Proc.?
INFO.	Task?	Miss.?	Flow?

PROCESS
TASKS
IDENTIFIED

3. Identify Management
Tasks

2. Identify Supervisory
Tasks

1. Identify Delivery
Tasks

REMEMBER . . .

	PLAN	PRODUCE	ASSESS
MGMT.	Tasks	Tasks	Tasks
SUPER.	Tasks	Tasks	Tasks
DEL.	Tasks	Tasks	Tasks

ANALYZING CONTEXTUAL TASKS

Job Aids

JOB AID

IDENTIFYING PROCESS TASKS

KEY RESULT AREA:

	PLAN	PRODUCE	ASSESS
MANAGEMENT			
SUPERVISORY			
DELIVERY			

IDENTIFYING PROCESS TASKS

KEY RESULT AREA:
Train supervisory personnel to improve on-the-job performance.

	PLAN	PRODUCE	ASSESS
MANAGEMENT	• Develop Goals for Industrial Relations (IR) Division • Make Strategic Decisions Regarding Overall Direction for IR • Develop 2-Year Strategic Plan • Develop Fiscal Year Budget for IR	• Present Budget and Strategic Plans to Corporate Board • Implement Strategic Plan for IR • Provide Direction to Supervisory IR Personnel	• Track IR Results Every Two Weeks • Monitor Monthly IR Expenditures • Conduct Annual Assessment of IR's Contribution to Mission • Conduct Biannual Performance Appraisal of Supervisory Personnel
SUPERVISORY	• Develop Work Plan and Goals for Professional Development Unit • Develop Task Assignments for ISD Personnel • Organize Weekly Assignments for ISD Personnel • Diagnose Skills/Knowledge of Current ISD Personnel	• Coordinate and Control Resource Utilization • Review and Direct Instructional Designs • Review and Direct Instructional Deliveries • Provide Technical Assistance to ISD Staff • Fill in for ISD Staff When Necessary	• Track Training Results at Completion of All Sessions • Monitor Resource Expenditures for Each Training Session • Assess Quality of Each Training Delivery • Assess Fulfillment of Unit Work Plan and Goals • Conduct Biannual Appraisal of ISD Personnel
DELIV	• Establish Productivity Goals for Supervisors to be Trained • Analyze Contextual Tasks • Specify Training Objectives • Develop Skill Content	• Develop Supervisory Training Materials • Produce Evaluation Instruments • Deliver Supervisory Skills Training	• Evaluate Process, Acquisition, Application, Transfer, and Productivity • Transmit Results and New Training Technologies

Specify Key Result Area
NOTE: This instructional design is for the Training Office. The goal is to improve supervisory training programs while cutting training costs.

List the delivery, supervisory, and management tasks of the area to receive training. NOTE: Since the example deals with improving a training program, we look at training personnel. If the instructional intervention was to improve line production, we would analyze personnel from the assembly plant.

ASSESSING CONTEXTUAL BARRIERS

	PHYSICAL	EMOTIONAL	INTELLECTUAL

P E R S O N N E L	CAPACITY
	☐ Lack of Strength
	☐ Lack of Dexterity
	☐ Lack of Stamina
	☐ Lack of Attentiveness
	☐ Lack of Concentration
	☐ Inability to Learn
	   New Tasks
		MOTIVES
		☐ Lack of Internalized
		   Reward System
		☐ Lack of Personalized
		   Goals
		☐ Lack of Initiative
		☐ Personnel Values
		   Inconsistent With
		   Mission
			SKILLS/KNOWLEDGE
			☐ Lack of Basic Skills
			☐ Lack of Specific Task-
			   Related Skills
			☐ Inadequate Knowledge
			   of Procedures and
			   Policies
			☐ Inadequate Understand-
			   ing of Supportive
			   Knowledge

E N V I R O N M E N T	RESOURCES
	☐ Inadequate Personnel
	☐ Inadequate Raw
	   Materials
	☐ Inadequate Supplies
	☐ Inadequate Equipment
	☐ Inadequate Space
	☐ Inadequate Support
	   Services
	☐ Inadequate Energy
		INCENTIVES
		☐ Good Performance Is
		   Not Positively
		   Reinforced
		☐ Poor Performance Is
		   Positively
		   Reinforced
		☐ Poor Performance Is
		   Not Linked to
		   Negative Conse-
		   quences
			PROCEDURES/METHODS
			☐ Out-of-Date Materials
			☐ Unreasonable Deadlines
			☐ Unclear Chain of
			   Command
			☐ Unclear Reporting
			   Structure
			☐ Lack of Access to
			   Decision Process
			☐ Work Not Oriented to
			   Performers
			☐ Extensive Paperwork/
			   Red Tape

I N F O R M A T I O N	TASK EXPECTATIONS
	☐ Inconsistent Task
	   Requirements
	☐ Conflicting Time
	   Demands
	☐ Inadequate Task
	   Assignment
	☐ Unnecessarily Com-
	   plex Tasks
	☐ Duplicative Task
	   Assignments
	☐ Infrequently Used
	   Tasks
		MISSION
		☐ No Policy
		☐ Conflicting Policies
		☐ Changing Policies
		☐ Conflicting Assign-
		   ment
		☐ Organizational Goals
		   Inconsistent With
		   Mission
			INFORMATION FLOW
			☐ Changing Information
			☐ Lack of Information
			☐ Lack of Accurate Data
			☐ Lack of Timely Data
			☐ Lack of Complete Data
			☐ Lack of Feedback
			☐ Lack of Monitoring

NOTE: These checks can be used when assessing contextual barriers at any level within the organization.

SPECIFYING TRAINING OBJECTIVES

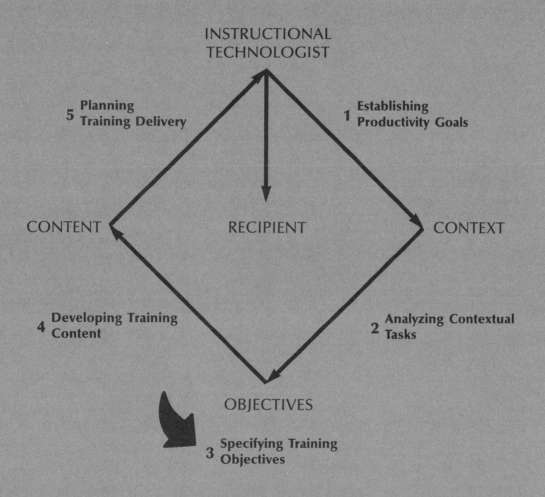

INSTRUCTIONAL
TECHNOLOGIST

5 Planning
Training Delivery

1 Establishing
Productivity Goals

CONTENT   RECIPIENT   CONTEXT

4 Developing Training
Content

2 Analyzing Contextual
Tasks

OBJECTIVES

3 Specifying Training
Objectives

> THE REMOVAL OF CONTEXTUAL BARRIERS REQUIRES
> THAT SPECIFIC OBJECTIVES BE ESTABLISHED

**What Is An
Objective?**

The analysis of contextual tasks told us where we are or where we need to be. The analysis defined the contextual tasks which relate to the pursuit of our productivity goals. We also assessed the barriers to task performance. We now need a precise definition of the training intervention objectives. Training objectives tell us what the recipients need to <u>do</u> to get from where they are to where they need to be.

**Why Specify
Objectives?**

We specify training intervention objectives in order to link the content of the training to the contextual requirements. Our objectives tell us what the training intervention needs to accomplish so that contextual tasks can be performed. The performance of these tasks will then lead to the achievement of the productivity goals. These assumptions can be summarized as follows:

- IF THE TRAINING ADDRESSES THESE OBJECTIVES, THEN CRITICAL TASKS CAN BE PERFORMED IN THE WORK SETTING.

- IF THE CRITICAL TASKS ARE PERFORMED IN THE WORK SETTING, THEN THE PRODUCTIVITY GOALS WILL BE REACHED.

It is similar to links in a chain. If one link is weak, the entire chain may be useless. If the contextual analysis or the training objectives are weak, then the training may not meet the productivity goal.

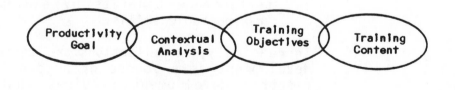

**When Are
Objectives
Specified?**

Training objectives are specified following the analysis of contextual tasks and prior to developing the training content. Training objectives are specified when the results of the barrier analysis indicate that an instructional intervention is needed.

**What Types Of
Training
Objectives
Are Specified?**

There are two types of training objectives, including:

- TASK OBJECTIVES: Those objectives that focus primarily on the performance of specific contextual tasks. For example, a task objective would be established when the primary purpose of a training session is to provide instruction on communicating work assignments.

- SKILL OBJECTIVES: Those objectives that focus on the skills or behavioral objectives underlying the performance of contextual tasks. For example, interpersonal skills such as attending, responding, personalizing, and initiating are underlying skills used when communicating work assignments. If the instructional intervention was to address the acquisition of interpersonal skills, then skill objectives would be set in addition to the task objectives.

**When Are Skill
Objectives
Specified?**

Task objectives are established for all instructional interventions that are designed to impact the work context. In addition to the task objectives, skill objectives are specified when:

- The task objectives can be reduced into meaningful skills.

- The intent of the training is to derive long-term performance benefits by equipping personnel with transportable skills.

Increasingly, organizations are emphasizing human resource development as a source of productivity growth. Human resource development requires that training programs emphasize person-specific skills development.

What Is Included In An Objective?

A fully defined training objective will include components, functions, processes, conditions, and standards. A training objective describes the following: who will do what, by what means and using what items, under what conditions, and to what standards.

TRAINING OBJECTIVES

<u>COMPONENTS</u>:	Who and what things are involved?	
<u>FUNCTIONS</u>:	What will be done?	
<u>PROCESSES</u>:	How will it be done?	
<u>CONDITIONS</u>:	Where, when, and why will it be done?	
<u>STANDARDS</u>:	How well will it be done?	

How Are Objectives Specified?

The following steps are completed when specifying training objectives:

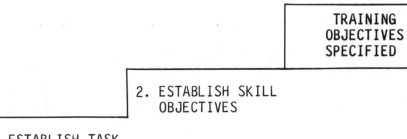

TRAINING
OBJECTIVES
SPECIFIED

2. ESTABLISH SKILL
OBJECTIVES

1. ESTABLISH TASK
OBJECTIVES

STEP 1: ESTABLISH TASK OBJECTIVES

What Are Task Objectives?

A task objective more fully defines the process tasks identified during the contextual analysis. This expanded task definition establishes the terminal behaviors expected of training recipients upon completion of the training. The ingredients of a task objective include components, functions, processes, conditions, and standards.

Why Establish Task Objectives?

Task objectives guide the development of the training content. In addition, the task objectives set expectations for the training recipients.

How Are Task Objectives Established?

The following substeps are completed when establishing task objectives:

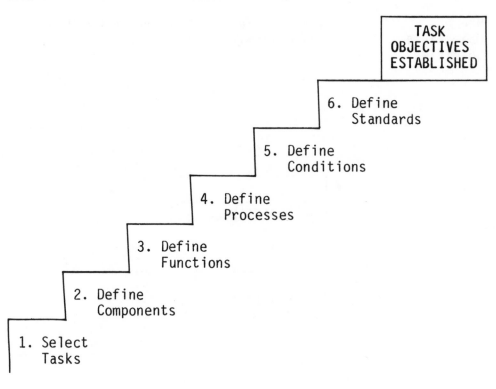

Substep 1:
Select Tasks

The first substep is to determine which process tasks will be included in the instructional intervention. The instructional intervention should include all tasks affected by the skills/knowledge barrier.

	PLAN	PRODUCE	ASSESS
MANAGEMENT	Tasks	Tasks	Tasks
SUPERVISORY	Tasks	Tasks	Tasks
DELIVERY	Tasks	Tasks	Tasks

Review the tasks in each cell. If the tasks contribute to the barrier, then they should be included in the instructional intervention.

Substep 2:
Define
Components

Once we have determined which tasks are to be included in the instructional intervention, then we begin defining the task objective by specifying the components. The components of a task objective are always nouns describing persons, data, or things involved in performing the task. The most important component in any task objective is the person who needs to acquire and perform the task. Sometimes components also include other things such as tools, special materials, machinery, or computers.

Examples

The following examples illustrate how components are defined:

1. **Components:**   The supervisory trainees . . .

2. **Components:**   Given the productivity goals and data from the contextual analysis, the ISD trainees . . .

Substep 3:
Define
Functions

Next we define functions. The functions of a task objective describe the desired behaviors that the training recipients will perform. The functions are always verbs that describe the desired behavioral outcomes of the instructional intervention.

Examples

The following examples illustrate how functions are defined:

1. **Components:**   The supervisory trainees
    Functions: will make work assignments . . .

2. **Components:**   Given the productivity goals and data from the contextual analysis, the ISD trainees
    Functions: will specify training objectives . . .

Substep 4:
Define
Processes

The fourth substep is to specify the processes. Processes are the means by which the task is performed. The processes are always adverbs that modify the functions of the objective. Usually, the description of the means is a straight-forward account of the activities necessary to achieve the desired behavioral outcomes. Sometimes special methods or alternative procedures are described.

Examples

The following examples illustrate how processes are defined:

1. **Components:**   The supervisory trainees
    Functions: will make work assignments
    Processes: by analyzing work unit objectives, designating responsibilities and tasks, setting timelines, and identifying the expected levels of effort. . .

2. **Components:**   Given the productivity goals and data from the contextual analysis, the ISD trainees
    Functions: will specify training objectives
    Processes: by defining components, functions, processes, conditions and standards. . .

Important Note

The inclusion of the processes in the training objectives is extremely important. The key to worker productivity in the Information Age is the worker's ability to process. Increasingly, instructional designers will need to teach both processes and outcomes.

Substep 5:
Define
Conditions

Once components, functions, and processes have been determined, then we define the conditions under which the task objective will be performed. Conditions are <u>adverbial</u> phrases which tell us:

- **Where**: The "where" tells us the context in which the task takes place. Understanding the context is important as the training recipients start to transfer their learnings from the training environment to other environments such as the work setting.

- **When**: The "when" tells us the beginning and end of the timeline for performing the task. Timelines also tell us when to observe or measure the behavior to determine if the objective has been achieved.

- **Why**: The "why" tells us the purposes to be achieved by training recipients when performing the tasks.

Examples

The following examples illustrate defining conditions:

1. **Components:** The supervisory trainees
    Functions: will make work assignments
    Processes: by analyzing work unit objectives, designating responsibilities and tasks, setting timelines, and identifying the expected levels of effort
    Conditions: before and during job performance to prevent crises . . .

Continued . . .

Examples
  (Continued)

2. Components: Given the productivity goals and data from the contextual analysis, the ISD trainees

Functions: will specify training objectives

Processes: by defining components, functions, processes, conditions, and standards

Conditions: after conducting a contextual analysis and before establishing training content so that training objectives relate to productivity goals. . .

Substep 6:
  Define
  Standards

The final substep is to define the standards. Standards are adverbial phrases which describe the desired level of excellence to be achieved. Standards may be absolute or relative.

- ABSOLUTE STANDARDS: Absolute standards are all or nothing. For example, an absolute standard for the Apollo Space Program was getting a person to the moon and back in good health.

- RELATIVE STANDARDS: Relative standards set the expected level of performance by describing the number or percentage of correction actions or responses.

Most often, relative standards are set during the acquisition stage of training. Absolute standards. may be appropriate in the presence of certain behaviors or responses.

Examples

The following examples illustrate how standards are defined:

1. Components: The supervisory trainees
    Functions: will make work assignments
    Processes: by analyzing work unit objectives, designating responsibilities and tasks, setting timelines, and identifying the expected levels of effort
    Conditions: before and during job performance to prevent crises
    Standards: at a level where employees can identify and carry out tasks on time at the expected level of performance.

ABSOLUTE
STANDARD

Continued . . .

90

Examples
(Continued)

2. <u>Components</u>:   Given the productivity goals and data from the contextual analysis, the ISD trainees

<u>Functions</u>:   will specify training objectives

<u>Processes</u>:   by defining components, functions, processes, conditions, and standards

<u>Conditions</u>:   after conducting a contextual analysis and before establishing training content so that training objectives relate to productivity goals

<u>Standards</u>:   at a 90% level of accuracy as measured by a master trainer.

**RELATIVE
STANDARD**

```
┌─────────────────────────────────────────────────────────┐
│                                                         │
│         STEP 2:  ESTABLISH SKILL OBJECTIVES             │
│                                                         │
└─────────────────────────────────────────────────────────┘
```

**What Are Skill
Objectives?**

A skill objective identifies the skills or behavioral activities underlying the performance of the contextual tasks. Employee behaviors can be classified into the following levels:

LEVEL 1: Duties or responsibilities

LEVEL 2: Tasks performed to discharge the duties

LEVEL 3: Skills comprising the tasks

Skill objectives address the third level of employee behaviors.

**Why Are Skill
Objectives
Important?**

Usually, instructional designers address employee behavior at the task level. However, increasing emphasis has begun to be placed on the instruction of behaviors at the skill level. This change in emphasis is due to the fact that job requirements are becoming less and less stable. Personnel who have acquired skill behaviors rather than task behaviors are more likely to transfer their skills from one set of job requirements to another. Therefore, skill training results in much greater long-term benefits for the employee and the organization.

```
┌─────────────────────────────────────────────────────────┐
│                                                         │
│         SKILLS ARE TRANSFERRABLE ASSETS                │
│                                                         │
└─────────────────────────────────────────────────────────┘
```

**When Are Skill
Objectives
Specified?**

As stated previously, skill objectives are specified when:

- The task objective can be reduced into meaningful skills.

- The intent of the training is to derive long-term performance benefits by equipping personnel with transportable skills.

When Are Skill Objectives Not Desirable?

Skill objectives may not be desirable when the intent of the training is to overcome an immediate performance problem. Skill objectives emphasize the acquisition of small units of employee behaviors, and therefore require more intensive training than typically provided when task objectives are specified. If the mandate is for a quick fix, then establishing skill objectives may not be desirable.

How Are Skill Objectives Established?

The following substeps are completed when establishing skill objectives:

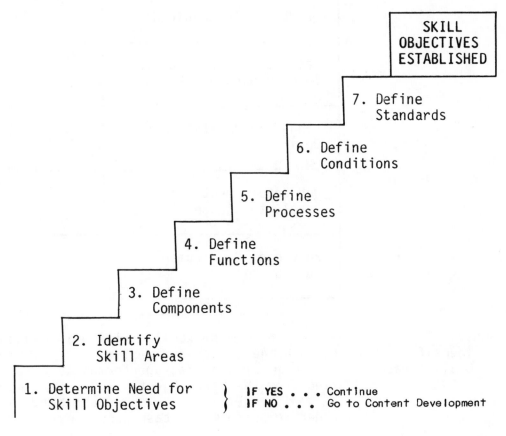

SKILL
OBJECTIVES
ESTABLISHED

7. Define
   Standards

6. Define
   Conditions

5. Define
   Processes

4. Define
   Functions

3. Define
   Components

2. Identify
   Skill Areas

1. Determine Need for
   Skill Objectives

IF YES . . . Continue
IF NO . . . Go to Content Development

Substep 1:
Determine Need
For Skill
Objectives

The first substep is to determine if skill objectives should be set in addition to the task objectives. Instructional designers make this determination by reviewing the productivity goals, data from the contextual analysis, and specific work unit mandates. The following guidelines can be used when determining if skill objectives are desirable:

IF . . .	THEN ESTABLISH SKILL OBJECTIVES?
Quick Fix is Required	No
Tasks Cannot Be Reduced Into Meaningful Skills	No
Long-Term Benefits Are Desired	Yes
Job Requirements are Likely to Change	Yes
Personnel Development is Valued	Yes

Substep 2:
Identify
Skill Areas

If we determine that skill objectives will indeed be established, then our next substep is to identify the skill areas underlying task performance. Skill areas are identified from the task objectives by reviewing the processes. We ask ourselves: "What skill behaviors are required in order to perform the task processes?"

Continued . . .

Substep 2:
  (Continued)

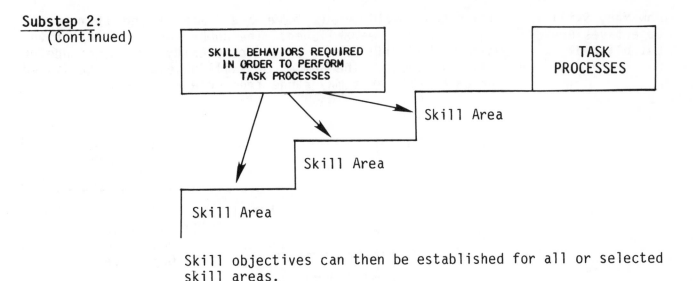

Skill objectives can then be established for all or selected skill areas.

Example

The following example illustrates how skill areas are identified for a task objective specified in the previous step.

TASK OBJECTIVE

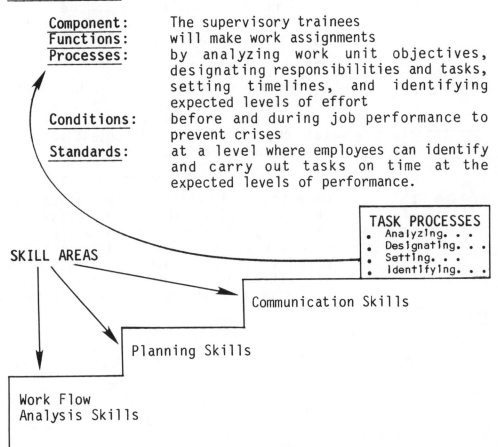

Component:	The supervisory trainees
Functions:	will make work assignments
Processes:	by analyzing work unit objectives, designating responsibilities and tasks, setting timelines, and identifying expected levels of effort
Conditions:	before and during job performance to prevent crises
Standards:	at a level where employees can identify and carry out tasks on time at the expected levels of performance.

TASK PROCESSES
• Analyzing. . .
• Designating. . .
• Setting. . .
• Identifying. . .

SKILL AREAS

Communication Skills

Planning Skills

Work Flow
Analysis Skills

How Many Skill Objectives Are Established?

After the skill areas have been identified then skill objectives are established. The number of skill objectives established will depend on the complexity and importance of the skill areas. The number of skill objectives established for each skill area may range from none to several.

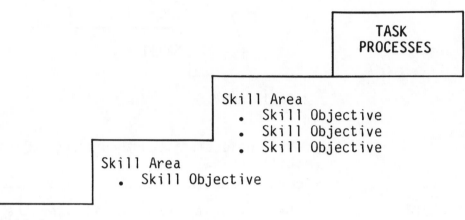

In the above illustration, no skill objectives will be established for Skill Area 1, one skill objective will be established for Skill Area 2, and three skill objectives will be established for Skill Area 3.

Note

The remaining substeps will be covered briefly since they are similar to the substeps used to define task objectives. Each substep will be reviewed. Any differences between how task objectives and skill objectives are established will be pointed out under each substep.

Substep 3: Define Components

Once the skill areas are identified, then the components of the skill objectives are specified. The components of a skill objective are identical to the components of a task objective. Remember, components are nouns describing persons, data, or things involved in the performance of the skill behavior. The primary components in any skill objective must be the recipients of the training experience.

Substep 4:
  Define
  Functions

Next, we define the functions of the skill objectives. The functions of a skill objective are verbs that describe the desired <u>skill</u> behaviors that the training recipients will be able to <u>do</u> at the completion of training. Remember, when establishing skill objectives, the functions must be expressed in terms of a skill behavior rather than a task behavior.

Example

The following example indicates the difference between a task behavior and a skill behavior.

<u>TASK BEHAVIOR</u>:   Communicate Assignments

<u>SKILL BEHAVIOR</u>:   Attend to Employees When Communicating Assignments

Substep 5:
  Define
  Processes

The fifth substep is to define the processes used to perform the skill. Processes are the means or skill steps used to achieve the desired skill outcomes.

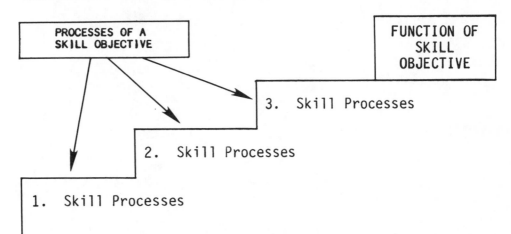

Example

The following example illustrates how processes are defined in skill objectives.

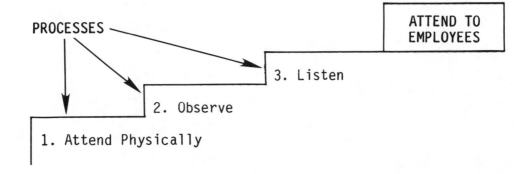

Substep 6:
Define
Conditions

Next, we define the conditions of the skill objective. The process used to identify the conditions of the skill objective is identical to the one used to define the conditions of a task objective. Remember, conditions are adverbial phrases which state where, when, and why the skill is performed.

Substep 7:
Define
Standards

The final substep is to define the standard or the level of excellence expected. Standards established for skill objectives are similar to those developed for task objectives. Measurable standards are expressed in either absolute or relative terms.

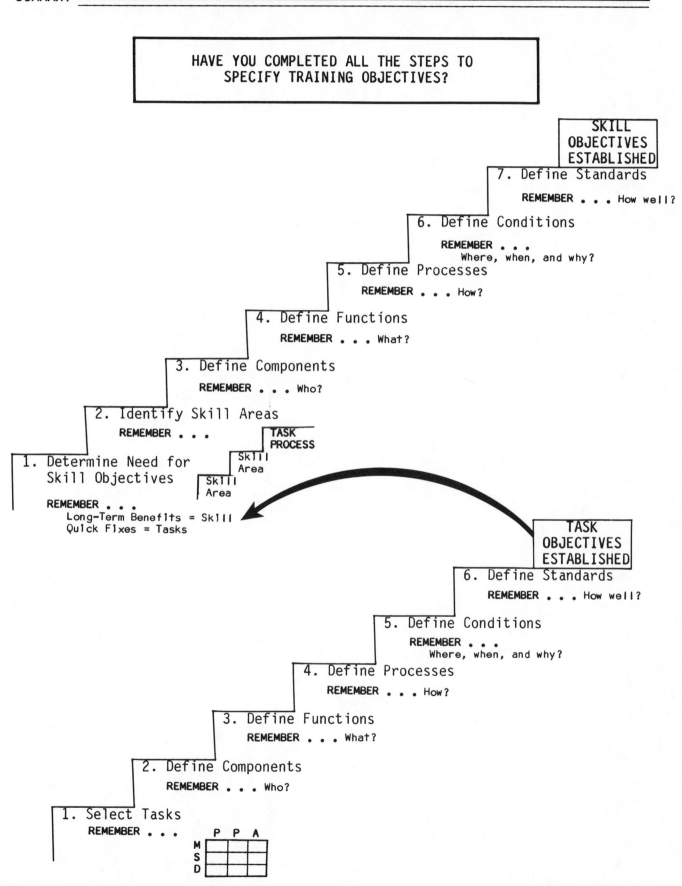

HAVE YOU COMPLETED ALL THE STEPS TO
SPECIFY TRAINING OBJECTIVES?

SKILL
OBJECTIVES
ESTABLISHED

7. Define Standards

REMEMBER . . . How well?

6. Define Conditions

REMEMBER . . .
Where, when, and why?

5. Define Processes

REMEMBER . . . How?

4. Define Functions

REMEMBER . . . What?

3. Define Components

REMEMBER . . . Who?

2. Identify Skill Areas

REMEMBER . . .

TASK
PROCESS

Skill
Area

1. Determine Need for
Skill Objectives

Skill
Area

REMEMBER . . .
Long-Term Benefits = Skill
Quick Fixes = Tasks

TASK
OBJECTIVES
ESTABLISHED

6. Define Standards

REMEMBER . . . How well?

5. Define Conditions

REMEMBER . . .
Where, when, and why?

4. Define Processes

REMEMBER . . . How?

3. Define Functions

REMEMBER . . . What?

2. Define Components

REMEMBER . . . Who?

1. Select Tasks

REMEMBER . . .

	P	P	A
M			
S			
D			

SPECIFYING TRAINING OBJECTIVES

Job Aids

SPECIFYING TRAINING OBJECTIVES

	TRAINING OBJECTIVE	TRAINING OBJECTIVE	TRAINING OBJECTIVE
COMPONENTS			
FUNCTIONS			
PROCESSES			
CONDITIONS			
STANDARDS			

SPECIFYING TRAINING OBJECTIVES

	TRAINING OBJECTIVE	QUESTIONS ANSWERED
COMPONENTS	Systems analyst trainees	Who and what things are involved?
FUNCTIONS	Will design physical (hard-ware) system for multiple users	What will be done?
PROCESSES	By identifying the tasks to be implemented by the system, analyzing the tasks, and determining requirements for input devices, output devices, central processing unit, mass storage, and communication	How will it be done?
CONDITIONS	While working within a variety of different time and cost constraints so that all the values for all users are met	Where, when, and why will it be done?
STANDARDS	At a level where the physical system meets the needs of 95% of all specified users as measured by the users' ability to implement the identified tasks under the agreed-upon conditions.	How well will it be done?

IDENTIFYING SKILL AREAS OR SKILL PROCESSES

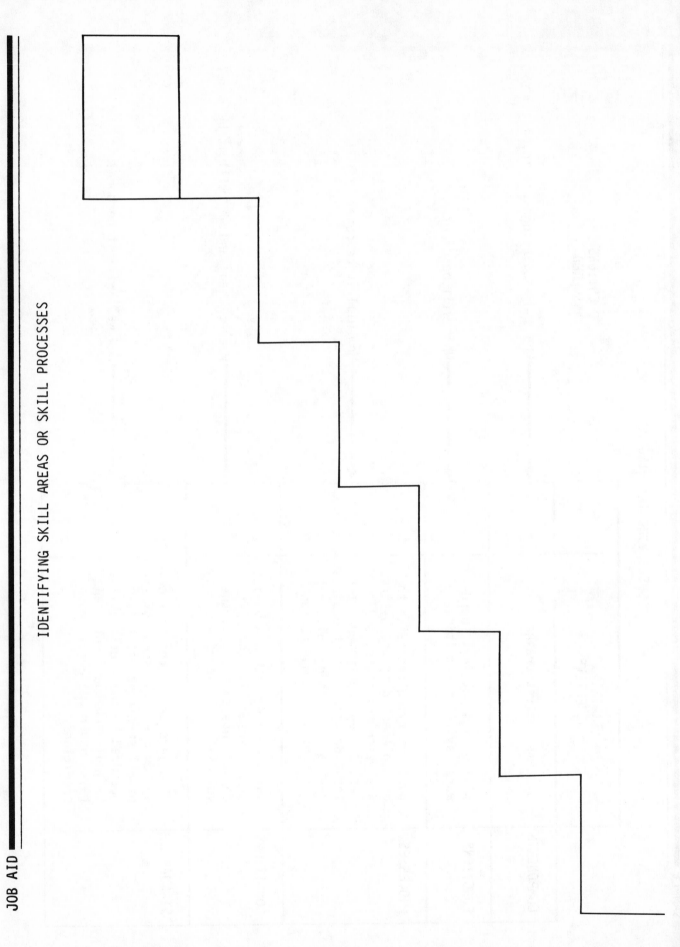

DEVELOPING
TRAINING
CONTENT

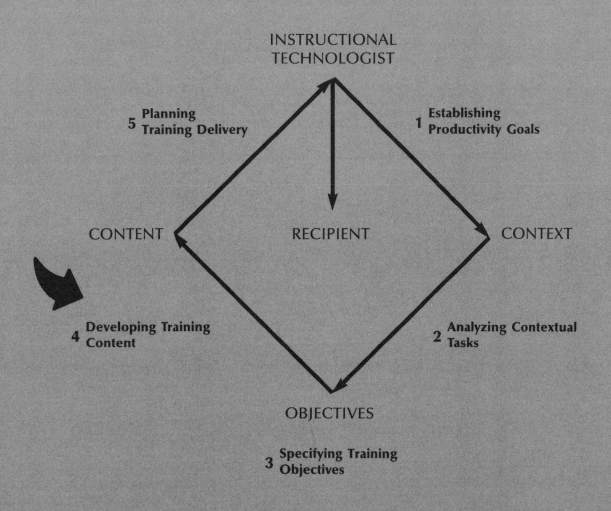

INSTRUCTIONAL
TECHNOLOGIST

5 Planning
Training Delivery

1 Establishing
Productivity Goals

CONTENT   RECIPIENT   CONTEXT

4 Developing Training
Content

2 Analyzing Contextual
Tasks

OBJECTIVES

3 Specifying Training
Objectives

┌───┐
│   THE ATTAINMENT OF YOUR TRAINING OBJECTIVES   │
│   DEPENDS ON THE QUALITY OF THE TRAINING CONTENT   │
└───┘

What Is Content Development?

The training objectives state what we are trying to accomplish during our instructional intervention. Content development identifies the skill steps or task steps and knowledge required to achieve the training objectives.

Why Develop Content?

The training content represents the bridge that enables the training recipients to advance from their current levels of performance to the desired level of performance. Our training objectives help us understand what the training is intended to achieve. Content development identifies what needs to be learned. The content development step forms the basis for making the training delivery.

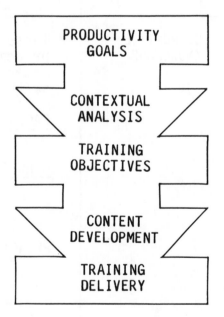

Remember, all of the steps in the instructional intervention process are linked to one another. Poor content development will result in poor training delivery.

When Is Content Developed?

Training content is developed after training objectives have been defined and before planning the training delivery.

What Is Included In The Training Content?

The following elements are included in the training content:

ELEMENT	EXPLANATION . . .
STEPS	Those behaviors which, when added together, will lead to the accomplishment of the training objectives.
SUBSTEPS	Those sub-behaviors which, when added together, will lead to the performance of a task/skill step.
SUPPORTIVE KNOWLEDGE	Those facts, concepts, and principles which are needed in order to perform a task or skill. FACTS: Describe the components, functions, and processes CONCEPTS: Describe the relationship among the components, functions, and processes. PRINCIPLES: Describe the implications of the components, functions, and processes

Figure 1 shows how the elements included in content development relate to one another.

Figure 1.

DEVELOPING TRAINING CONTENT

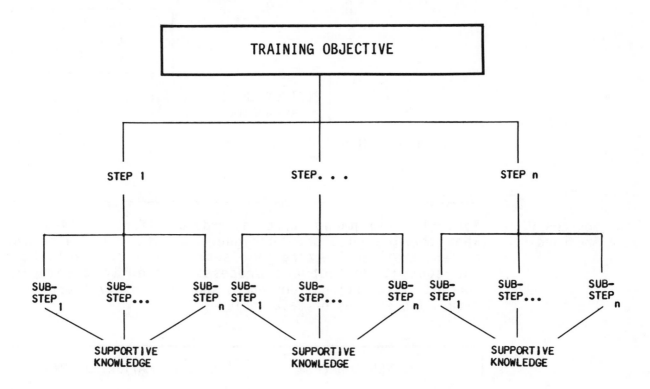

Explanation:

1. Task steps or skill steps are derived from each training objective by asking, "What behaviors will lead to the accomplishment of this objective?"

2. Each step is broken down into small, sequenced substeps that a person must do in order to perform the major step. The substeps must be broken down into units which trainees can successfully learn, practice, and master. Skill steps may be further broken down if the content is very complex.

3. Supportive knowledge may accompany each step or each substep. A comprehensive content will include facts, concepts, and principles for each step. When it is not possible to provide supportive knowledge for each step, then facts, concepts, and principles must be provided for each training objective.

How Is Training Content Developed?   The following steps are completed when developing the training content:

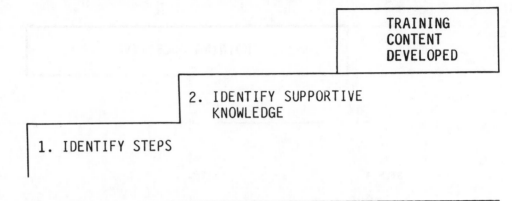

TRAINING
CONTENT
DEVELOPED

2. IDENTIFY SUPPORTIVE
   KNOWLEDGE

1. IDENTIFY STEPS

What Sources Of Data Are Used?   Content development can be an arduous effort, particularly when the instructional designer is unfamiliar with the content area. Collecting good source data can facilitate the content development process. Prior to developing content, instructional designers should identify sources of data. The sources of data include:

WRITTEN SOURCES	SUBJECT MATTER EXPERTS
• Regulations • Policy Statements • Legislation • Literature Reviews • Procedural Manuals • Related Training Curriculum	• Exemplary Performers • Supervisory Personnel • Experts Outside of the Organization

---

STEP 1: IDENTIFY STEPS

What Are Steps?

Steps constitute the follow-through program that is the basis for achieving the training objective. The steps may be either:

- **TASK STEPS:** We identify task steps or subtasks when our instructional intervention is limited to task objectives.

- **SKILL STEPS:** Skill steps are identified when our instructional intervention includes skill objectives.

The use of the term "step" refers to both task steps and skill steps. The same procedures are used to identify task steps and skill steps.

Why Are Steps Identified?

Instruction is most effective when the content is broken down into the smallest possible steps for presentation to the training recipients. The smaller the steps, the higher the probability that trainees will achieve the training objectives. Stated more simply, to leave out a step is to increase the probability that your training will fail.

What Types Of Steps Are Identified?

Steps include the activities that training recipients must do and things that training recipients must think about. The DO steps and THINK steps define the development of the steps that lead to achieving the training objective.

How Are Steps Identified?

The following substeps are completed when identifying task steps or skill steps:

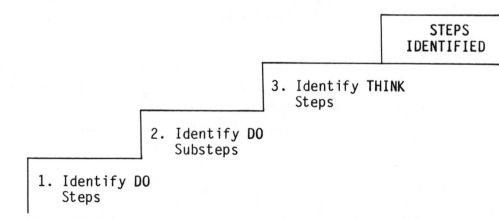

STEPS IDENTIFIED

3. Identify THINK Steps

2. Identify DO Substeps

1. Identify DO Steps

Substep 1:
Identify
DO Steps

The first substep is to identify the DO steps. DO steps are developed by listing the major steps that the trainee will need to do to perform the task or skill. The final steps should culminate in the achievement of the training objective. The intermediary steps guide the trainee to successful performance of the task or skill. One method for identifying steps is explained below. This method for identifying steps is particularly helpful when the steps are not self-evident.

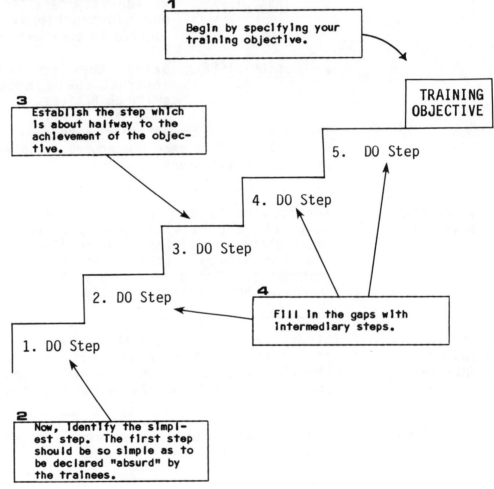

Example

Figure 2 on the following page illustrates how DO steps are identified.

Figure 2.

IDENTIFYING DO STEPS

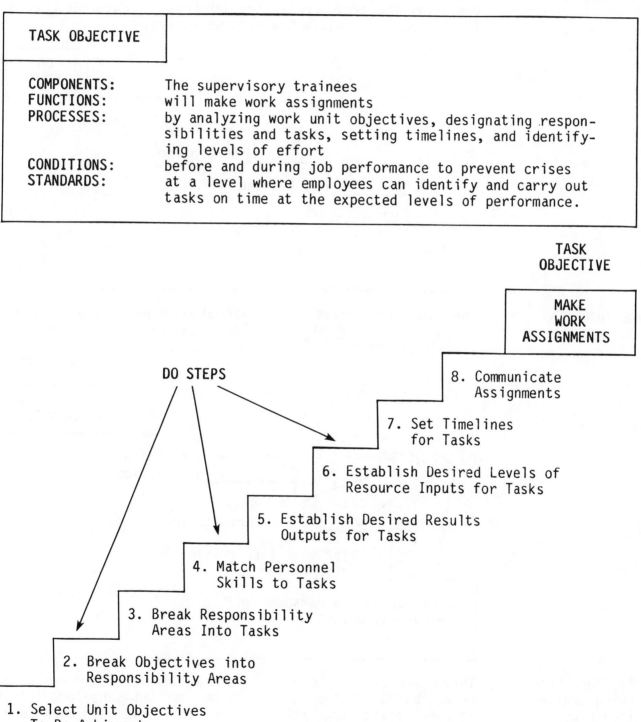

TASK OBJECTIVE

COMPONENTS:	The supervisory trainees
FUNCTIONS:	will make work assignments
PROCESSES:	by analyzing work unit objectives, designating responsibilities and tasks, setting timelines, and identifying levels of effort
CONDITIONS:	before and during job performance to prevent crises
STANDARDS:	at a level where employees can identify and carry out tasks on time at the expected levels of performance.

TASK
OBJECTIVE

MAKE
WORK
ASSIGNMENTS

DO STEPS

8. Communicate
   Assignments

7. Set Timelines
   for Tasks

6. Establish Desired Levels of
   Resource Inputs for Tasks

5. Establish Desired Results
   Outputs for Tasks

4. Match Personnel
   Skills to Tasks

3. Break Responsibility
   Areas Into Tasks

2. Break Objectives into
   Responsibility Areas

1. Select Unit Objectives
   To Be Achieved

Substep 2:
   **Identify DO
   Substeps**

The next step is to identify DO substeps. DO substeps are the sub-behaviors which, when added together, will lead to the performance of a DO step. DO substeps are developed in precisely the same way as the DO steps. Each DO step is treated as if it was a training objective.

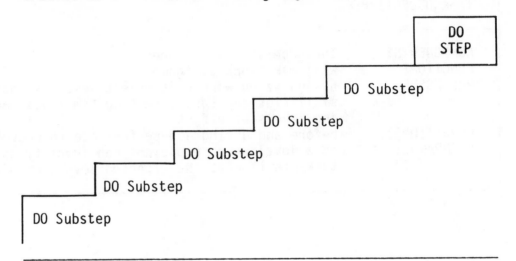

Example

The following example illustrates how DO substeps are identified for DO Step 8: Communicate Assignments from the example presented in Figure 2.

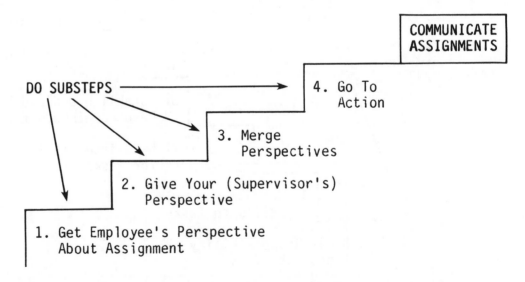

**Is There Some-
thing Smaller
Than A DO
Substep?**

There may be instances when it would be advantageous to break the DO substeps into even smaller sub-behaviors. This is particularly true when your objective has been defined at the task level. A further reduction of DO substeps is completed in a manner similar to the identification of steps and substeps.

Example

The following example demonstrates how <u>Substep 1</u>: Get Employee's Perspective About Assignments can be reduced into smaller sub-behaviors for instruction.

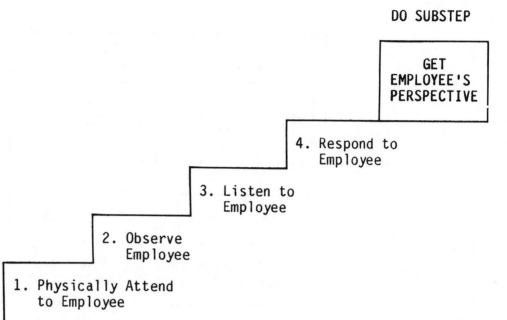

DO SUBSTEP

GET EMPLOYEE'S PERSPECTIVE

4. Respond to Employee

3. Listen to Employee

2. Observe Employee

1. Physically Attend to Employee

NOTE: A skill objective would be broken down into still smaller units of behavior.

When Is Content Small Enough?

The smaller the steps the better. Remember, at this point we are only developing the content. The trainee's potential reaction to the atomistic nature or simplicity of the steps should <u>not</u> affect your content development efforts. Substeps can always be recombined if the pace becomes a problem when planning the content presentation.

REMEMBER . . .

A disciplined approach to content development will free the instructional designer to be creative while planning the content delivery.

Substep 3:
 <u>Identify</u>
 <u>THINK Steps</u>

After identifying DO steps, we identify THINK steps. THINK steps help trainees <u>before</u>, <u>during</u>, and <u>after</u> completing a DO step or substep. To identify THINK steps, we answer the following questions about the performance of each DO step or substep:

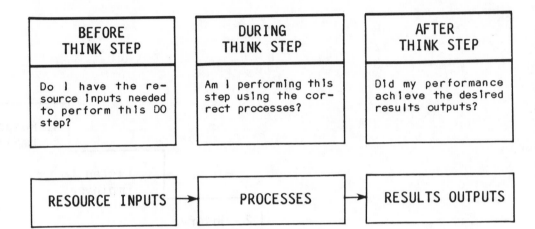

BEFORE THINK STEP	DURING THINK STEP	AFTER THINK STEP
Do I have the re-source inputs needed to perform this DO step?	Am I performing this step using the cor-rect processes?	Did my performance achieve the desired results outputs?

RESOURCE INPUTS → PROCESSES → RESULTS OUTPUTS

If the trainees know the THINK steps, then they can monitor their own performance on the DO steps.

Example

The following example illustrates how THINK steps are identified for <u>DO Step 8</u>: Communicate Assignments from the example presented in Figure 2.

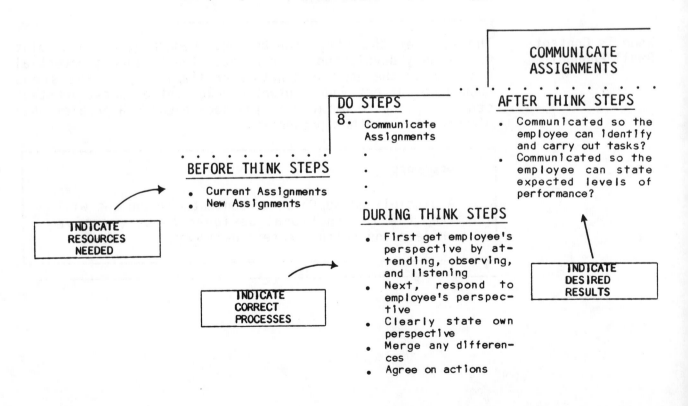

COMMUNICATE ASSIGNMENTS

DO STEPS
8. Communicate Assignments

BEFORE THINK STEPS
• Current Assignments
• New Assignments

DURING THINK STEPS
• First get employee's perspective by at-tending, observing, and listening
• Next, respond to employee's perspec-tive
• Clearly state own perspective
• Merge any differen-ces
• Agree on actions

AFTER THINK STEPS
• Communicated so the employee can identify and carry out tasks?
• Communicated so the employee can state expected levels of performance?

INDICATE RESOURCES NEEDED

INDICATE CORRECT PROCESSES

INDICATE DESIRED RESULTS

STEP 2: IDENTIFY SUPPORTIVE KNOWLEDGE

What Is Supportive Knowledge?

Knowledge is a necessary but <u>not</u> sufficient condition for acquiring a new task behavior or skill. Because we know about something does not necessarily mean we can do it. At the same time, knowledge about a process (i.e., task or skill) can support a trainee's achievement of a training objective. Supportive knowledge includes <u>facts</u>, <u>concepts</u>, and <u>principles</u>.

Why Is Supportive Knowledge Identified?

Knowledge is incorporated into the training content when it facilitates the acquisition of a task or skill. Supportive knowledge is most helpful when facts and concepts are integrated into principles that lead to training objectives. When training recipients know the principles, then they are more likely to acquire, apply, and transfer a task or skill behavior.

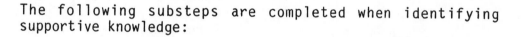

KNOWLEDGE SUPPORTS LEARNING ACQUISITION,
APPLICATION, AND TRANSFER

How Is Supportive Knowledge Identified?

The following substeps are completed when identifying supportive knowledge:

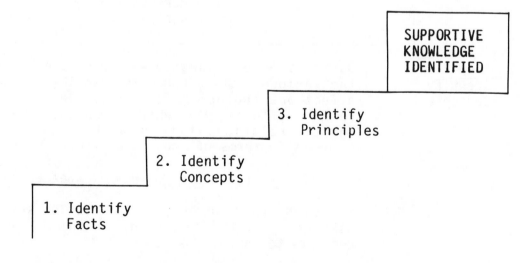

**Substep 1:
Identify
Facts**

The first substep is to identify the facts related to the task or skill objective. Facts name the components, functions, and processes of the training objective or step. The facts are related to the task or skill performance by asking:

- Does the training recipient need to know this fact to do this task or skill?

- Will knowing this fact help the training recipient to do this task or skill better?

Limiting the content to the supportive facts will make the training presentation more relevant.

Example

The following example illustrates how facts are identified.

DO STEP: COMMUNICATE ASSIGNMENTS

DO SUBSTEPS: Get Employee's Perspective about Assignments
                Give Your (Supervisor's) Perspective
                Merge Perspectives
                Go to Action

FACTS: Employee   } COMPONENTS
                Supervisor }
                Make Assignments   } FUNCTIONS
                Get Employee's Perspective
                Give Supervisor's Perspective   } PROCESSES
                Merge Perspectives
                Go to Action

**Substep 2:
Identify
Concepts**

During the next substep we explore the relationships among the various facts. Concepts describe how the various facts affect one another. Conceptual learning enables training recipients to organize what they know. One way of presenting the relationships among the facts is to express the concepts in terms of cause-and-effect relationships.

"IF _____(cause)_____, THEN _____(effect)_____."

We relate the concepts to the task or skill performance by asking: "Do the training recipients need to know the concepts to do the task or skill?"

Example

The following example illustrates how concepts are identified.

DO STEP: COMMUNICATE ASSIGNMENTS

DO SUBSTEPS: Get Employee's Perspective about Assignments
Give Your (Supervisor's) Perspective
Merge Perspectives
Go to Action

FACTS: Employees
Supervisors
Make Assignments
Get Employee's Perspective
Give Supervisor's Perspective
Merge Perspectives
Go to Action

CONCEPTS: If the supervisory trainee gets the employee's perspective, **then** the employee is more likely to accept the assignment.

If the supervisory trainee clearly gives his/her perspective, **then** the employee is more likely to understand the performance expectations.

If the supervisory trainee merges discrepant perspectives, **then** the potential for continued conflict will be reduced.

Substep 3:
Identify
Principles

The final substep is to identify the principles related to task or skill performance. Principles organize the facts and concepts around their purposes. There are many principles related to the content we teach. The most important principles describe how and why something works. Most principles deal with the implications of the cause-and-effect relationships of the concepts.

    "IF   (cause) , THEN   (effect) ,
    SO THAT   (implications)   ."

Like facts and concepts, principles take on significance in relation to the task or skill performance by asking: "Do the training recipients need to know the principle to perform the task or skill?"

Example   The following example illustrates how principles are identified.

DO STEP: COMMUNICATE ASSIGNMENTS

DO SUBSTEPS: Get Employee's Perspective about Assignments
Give Your (Supervisor's) Perspective
Merge Perspectives
Go to Action

FACTS: Employees
Supervisors
Make Assignments
Get Employee's Perspective
Give Supervisor's Perspective
Merge Perspectives
Go to Action

CONCEPTS: If the supervisory trainee gets the employee's perspective, **then** the employee is more likely to accept the assignment.

If the supervisory trainee clearly gives his/her perspective, **then** the employee will understand the work assignment.

If the supervisory trainee merges discrepant perspectives, **then** the potential for continued conflict will be reduced.

PRINCIPLES: If the supervisory trainee communicates with the employee when making assignments, **then** the employee can identify and carry out tasks on time at the expected level of performance **so that** work unit objectives can be achieved.

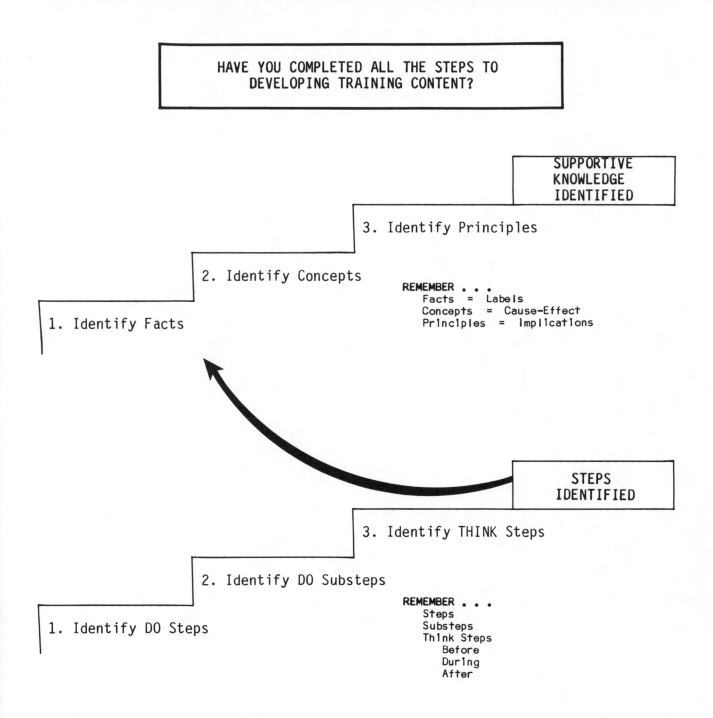

HAVE YOU COMPLETED ALL THE STEPS TO
DEVELOPING TRAINING CONTENT?

SUPPORTIVE
KNOWLEDGE
IDENTIFIED

3. Identify Principles

2. Identify Concepts

1. Identify Facts

REMEMBER . . .
Facts = Labels
Concepts = Cause-Effect
Principles = Implications

STEPS
IDENTIFIED

3. Identify THINK Steps

2. Identify DO Substeps

1. Identify DO Steps

REMEMBER . . .
Steps
Substeps
Think Steps
Before
During
After

DEVELOPING TRAINING CONTENT

Job Aids

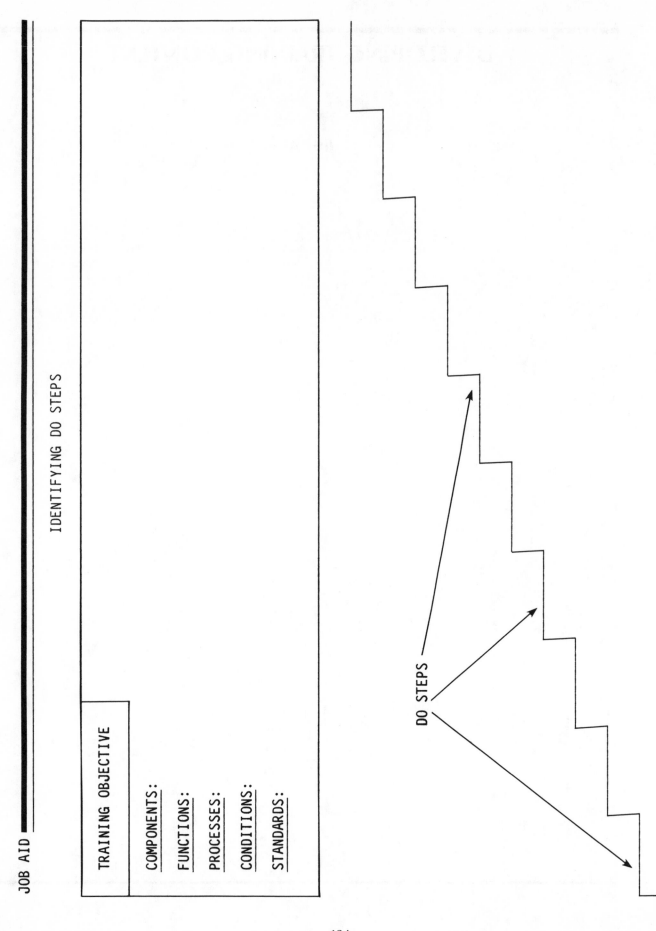

JOB AID

IDENTIFYING DO STEPS

TRAINING OBJECTIVE

COMPONENTS:

FUNCTIONS:

PROCESSES:

CONDITIONS:

STANDARDS:

DO STEPS

IDENTIFYING DO STEPS

TRAINING OBJECTIVE

COMPONENTS: ISD Interns
FUNCTIONS: will personalize trainees' learning experiences
PROCESSES: by relating the training content to individual trainee problems and learning goals
CONDITIONS: throughout the training process so that trainees will relate the training to their job tasks.
STANDARDS: Trainees will transfer 90% of their learnings to performance on the job.

1. Identify Individual Trainee Problems

2. Identify Individual Trainee Goals

3. Relate Training Content to Individual Individual Goals

DO STEPS

IDENTIFYING DO SUBSTEPS

DO STEP

DO SUBSTEPS

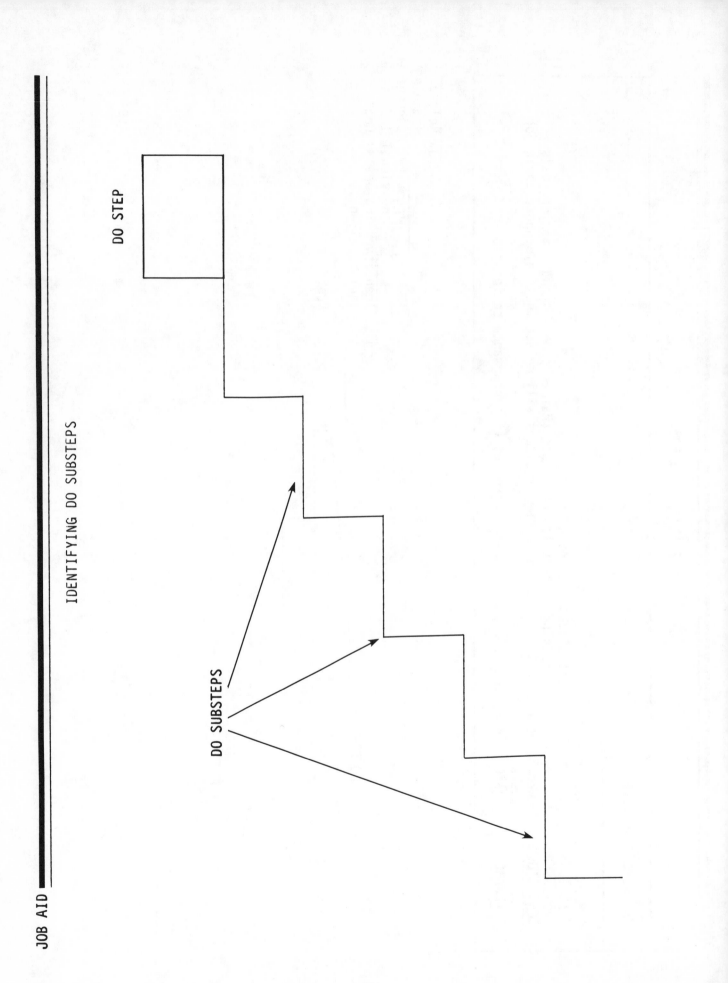

IDENTIFYING DO SUBSTEPS

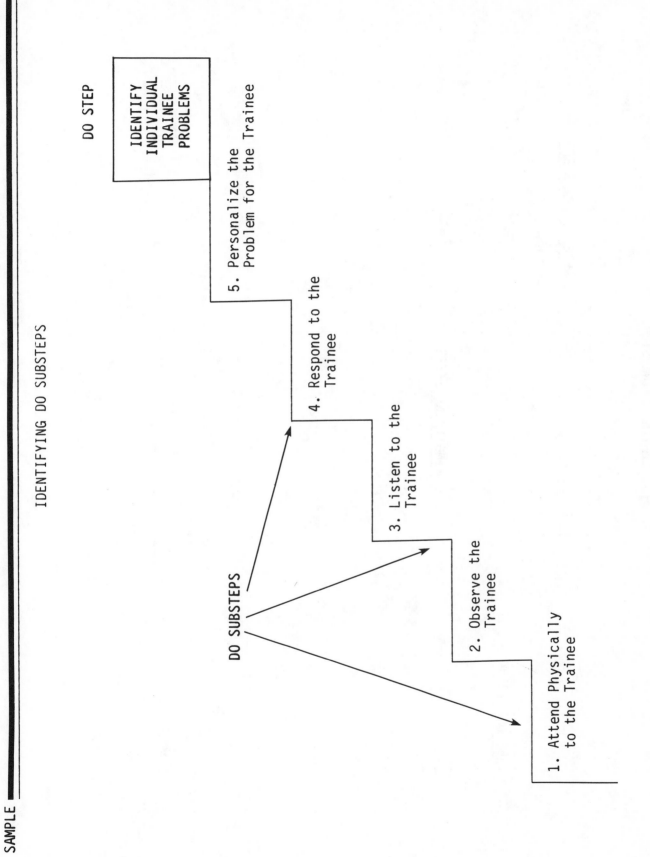

DO STEP

IDENTIFY
INDIVIDUAL
TRAINEE
PROBLEMS

5. Personalize the
Problem for the Trainee

4. Respond to the
Trainee

3. Listen to the
Trainee

2. Observe the
Trainee

1. Attend Physically
to the Trainee

DO SUBSTEPS

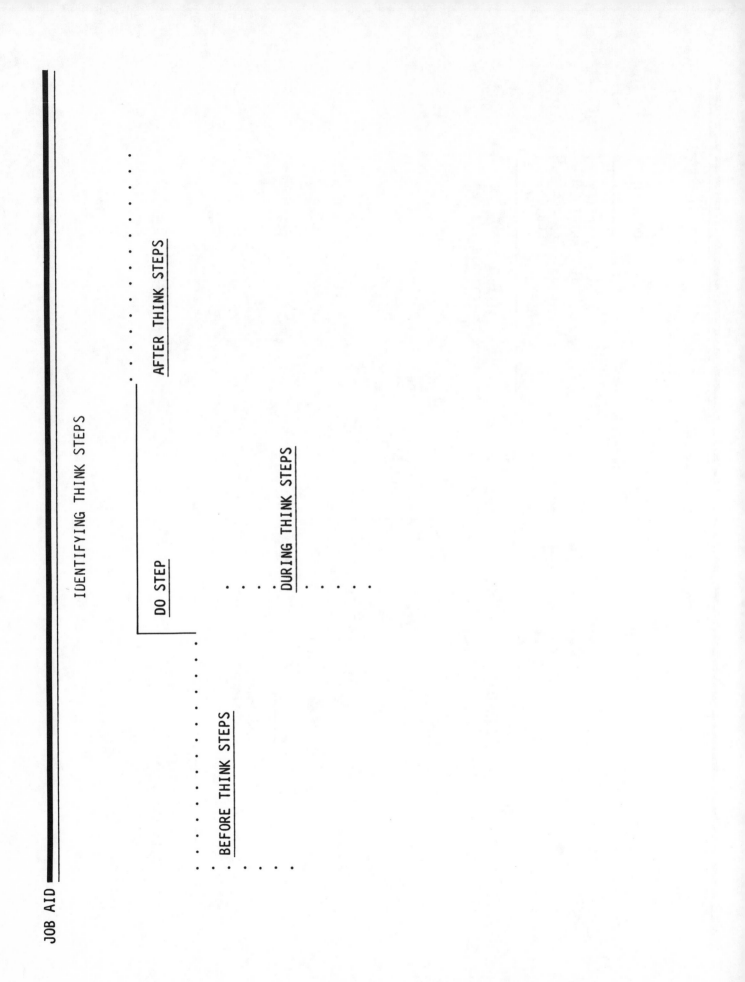

JOB AID

IDENTIFYING THINK STEPS

BEFORE THINK STEPS

DO STEP

DURING THINK STEPS

AFTER THINK STEPS

IDENTIFYING THINK STEPS

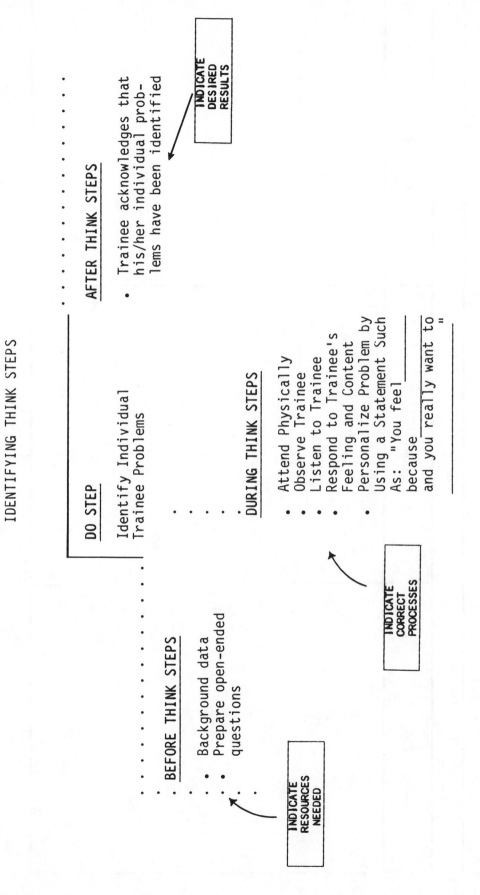

DO STEP

Identify Individual
Trainee Problems

AFTER THINK STEPS

• Trainee acknowledges that
  his/her individual problems have been identified

INDICATE
DESIRED
RESULTS

DURING THINK STEPS

• Attend Physically
• Observe Trainee
• Listen to Trainee
• Respond to Trainee's
  Feeling and Content
• Personalize Problem by
  Using a Statement Such
  As: "You feel
         because
  and you really want to
  "

INDICATE
CORRECT
PROCESSES

BEFORE THINK STEPS

• Background data
• Prepare open-ended
  questions

INDICATE
RESOURCES
NEEDED

IDENTIFYING SUPPORTIVE KNOWLEDGE

☐ STEPS
    OR :
☐ SUBSTEPS

FACTS	CONCEPTS	PRINCIPLES

IDENTIFYING SUPPORTIVE KNOWLEDGE

☑ STEPS
OR :
☐ SUBSTEPS

1. Identify Individual Trainee Problems
2. Identify Individual Trainee Goals
3. Relate Training Content to Individual Goals

FACTS	CONCEPTS	PRINCIPLES
Instructional Designer Trainees Personalization Trainee Problems Trainee Goals	If the trainer can identify the trainee's problem, then the trainer can assist the trainee in identifying a learning goal. If the trainee can relate his/her goal to the training content, then the trainee will have a reason to learn the training content.	If instructional designers personalize trainees' learning experiences, then the trainees will know specifically what they need to learn or improve so that on-the-job performance can be improved.

Indicate the Implications of the Facts and Concepts

State Cause and Effect Relationships Among Facts

Label the Components, Functions, and Processes

List Either Steps or Substeps

PLANNING
TRAINING
DELIVERY

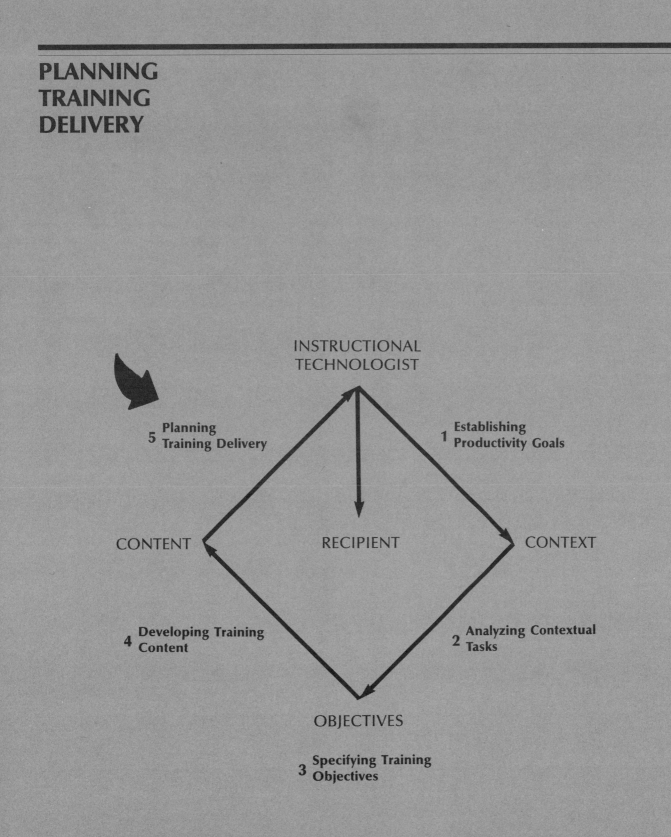

┌───┐
│ AN EFFECTIVE DELIVERY PLAN IS REQUIRED TO ENSURE   │
│ THAT OUR CONTENT WILL IMPACT THE RECIPIENTS   │
└───┘

What Is A Training Delivery Plan?

We have now developed our training content. We have identified our steps, substeps, and supportive knowledge. We now need to plan for our training delivery. A training delivery plan organizes the content and establishes the training methods.

Why Make A Training Delivery Plan?

The greatest contribution an instructional designer/technologist or trainer can make is to develop a plan for delivery that is responsive to the recipients' needs. A good intervention plan goes a long way toward ensuring successful instruction. A delivery plan links the content, the recipient, the instructional technologist, and the training objectives in a systematic yet dynamic fashion. The plan provides a written document that can be pilot tested, revised, validated, and transported so that others can replicate the training.

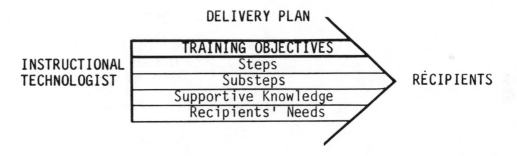

The delivery plan is the vehicle used by the instructional technologist to provide recipients with new tasks, skills, and knowledge.

What Is Included In A Training Delivery?

All effective training deliveries have the following components:

• <u>Systematic Organization</u>: Content is organized in a way which systematically provides recipients with new tasks, skills, and knowledge.

Continued . . .

What Is Included In A Training Delivery?
(Continued)

- <u>**Effective Methods/Media**</u>: Methods and media are used which ensure the delivery of the content.

- <u>**Interpersonal Skills**</u>: Instructors or materials attend and respond to the recipients' frames of reference.

What Should The Training Plan Include?

The training delivery plan organizes the content (i.e., steps, substeps, and supportive knowledge) and establishes the methods and media to be used when making the delivery. Wherever possible, interpersonal skills should also be built into the plan. This can be done by programming into the plan opportunities for the instructor to get the frame of reference of the recipients and respond to that frame of reference.

How Is Content Organized?

Content is organized in a way which facilitates the recipients' acquisition of new tasks, skills, and knowledge. This means that the following elements are present:

- <u>R</u>eview: Content is reviewed in order to get an index of what the recipients do and do not know about the content to be addressed.

- <u>O</u>verview: Content is overviewed in order to share images with the recipients on the content and its importance.

- <u>P</u>resentation: Content is presented so that recipients can learn the tasks or skills and accomplish the training objectives.

- <u>E</u>xercise: Exercises provide recipients with an opportunity to practice the tasks or skills.

- <u>S</u>ummary: Content is summarized in order to get an index of what the recipients do and do not know about the tasks or skills following the training delivery.

A helpful acronym for remembering content organization is <u>ROPES</u>. Planning the content delivery may be thought of as <u>ROPING</u> the content.

What Methods Are Used To Deliver The Content?

Within each phase of content organization (i.e., ROPES), the delivery plan should incorporate the following methods:

METHOD	WHAT IT DOES
Didactic (Telling)	Informs the recipients about what is to be done and how to do it.
Modeling (Showing)	Demonstrates to the recipients how to do it.
Exercise (Doing)	Provides recipients with the opportunity to do it.

Together, the TELL, SHOW, and DO methods equip the recipients with everything they need to perform the task or skill.

How Does ROPES And Tell, Show, Do Fit Together?

Tell, Show, and Do methods are used throughout the content delivery. Table 8 illustrates how Tell, Show, and Do methods are used in each phase of ROPES.

What Are Training Media?

Training media are the vehicles we use in order to deliver our training content. Examples of the most common categories of instructional media include:

- Audio
- Projected Still-Visual
- Print Materials
- Human Resources (i.e., (instructors, peers, etc.)

- Audio-Visual
- Motion-Visual
- Actual or Models of Objects
- Computers

An effective training delivery may draw on several different types of media.

Table 8.

THE TRAINING DELIVERY PROCESS

	TELL	SHOW	DO
REVIEW	Recipients tell what they know.	Recipients show what they know.	Recipients perform the tasks or skills they know.
OVERVIEW	Instructor and recipients tell their images of the content.	Instructor and recipients show each other the applications that they might make after the training.	Instructor and recipients demonstrate the applications that they might make after the training.
PRESENT	Instructor tells about the steps, substeps, and supportive knowledge.	Instructor shows the specific steps and substeps.	Recipients demonstrate the specific steps and substeps.
EXERCISE	Recipients tell out loud or to themselves about the steps, substeps, and supportive knowledge.	Recipients show how the specific steps can be used in a structured training activity.	Recipients do the specific steps in applications which are similar to on-the-job situations.
SUMMARY	Recipients tell about the steps, substeps, and supportive knowledge.	Recipients show how they will use the steps when they return to their work setting.	Recipients plan to do the specific steps in the work setting.

Where Does Media Fit In The Delivery Plan?

The selection of training media occurs within the ROPES x TELL, SHOW, DO structure. We select the appropriate media for the activities planned in each cell of the following matrix.

	TELL	SHOW	DO
REVIEW	Select Media	Select Media	Select Media
OVERVIEW	Select Media	Select Media	Select Media
PRESENT	Select Media	Select Media	Select Media
EXERCISE	Select Media	Select Media	Select Media
SUMMARY	Select Media	Select Media	Select Media

For example, the content delivery plan for a course on microcomputers might include the following media in the Exercise/Do cell:

- Computer-Assisted Drill and Practice
- Computer-Assisted Simulation
- Exercise on an Actual Microcomputer

How Is Training Delivery Planned?

The following steps are completed when planning the training delivery:

TRAINING
DELIVERY
PLANNED

2. SELECT TRAINING MEDIA

1. DEVELOP TRAINING ACTIVITIES

```
┌─────────────────────────────────────────────────────┐
│                                                       │
│         STEP 1:  DEVELOP TRAINING ACTIVITIES          │
│                                                       │
└─────────────────────────────────────────────────────┘
```

What Are Training Activities?

Training activities are the actions taken by the instructor (or instructional medium) and the training recipient. Training activities for the instructor and the training recipients are developed within each cell of the following matrix:

	TELL	SHOW	DO
REVIEW	Training Activities	Training Activities	Training Activities
OVERVIEW	Training Activities	Training Activities	Training Activities
PRESENT	Training Activities	Training Activities	Training Activities
EXERCISE	Training Activities	Training Activities	Training Activities
SUMMARY	Training Activities	Training Activities	Training Activities

Why Are Training Activities Important?

Training activities make the content come alive for the training recipients. The development of creative activities within the ROPES x TELL, SHOW, DO structure is the key to successful training delivery.

How Are Training
Activities
Developed?

The following substeps are completed when developing training activities:

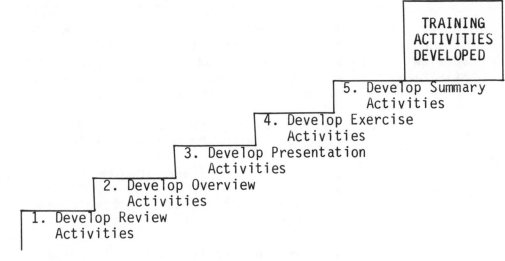

TRAINING
ACTIVITIES
DEVELOPED

5. Develop Summary
   Activities

4. Develop Exercise
   Activities

3. Develop Presentation
   Activities

2. Develop Overview
   Activities

1. Develop Review
   Activities

Substep 1:
   Develop Review
   Activities

The first type of training activities planned are the review activities. The review activities answer the question: "What other tasks, skills, or knowledge do our training recipients need to have before they can achieve the training objective?"

The review activities also give the instructor an opportunity to gauge the trainees' levels of functioning on contingency tasks or skills. Contingency tasks or skills are those required in order to perform the current training objective. For example, in order to write a correct sentence, trainees must be able to write, spell, and identify the subject and predicate. In summary, review activities permit us to determine where the training recipients are in relation to the content they are about to acquire.

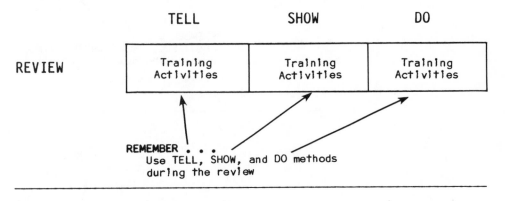

REVIEW

TELL
Training
Activities

SHOW
Training
Activities

DO
Training
Activities

REMEMBER . . .
Use TELL, SHOW, and DO methods
during the review

Example

Table 9, at the completion of this step, presents sample review activities.

Substep 2:
  Develop
  Overview
  Activities

At the completion of the review activities, we have a picture of where the training recipients are in relation to the content. Our next substep is to develop overview activities. During the overview, we develop a picture of where the training recipients want or need to be.

The overview provides both the instructor and training recipients with the opportunity to:

- Share their images of the training objectives.

- Reach a consensus about the reasons for acquiring the content.

- Relate training content to potential applications.

The overview activities should motivate the training recipients by developing the potential content applications and relating them to the content to be acquired. Applications are related to the training content through the presentation of principles. Overviewing the content should culminate with the development of principles.

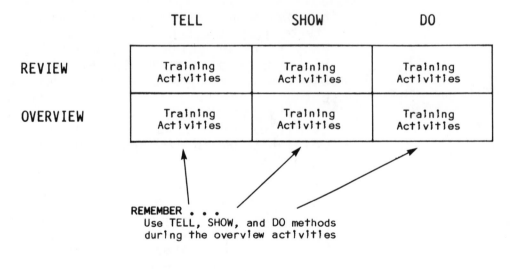

Example   Table 10, at the completion of this step, presents sample
                       overview activities.

Substep 3:   The next substep is to develop the presentation activities.
  Develop   The presentation is the "how to do it" part of the training
  Presentation   delivery.   Presentation activities include providing the
  Activities   training recipients with the steps, substeps, and supportive
                       knowledge needed to achieve the training objective. Remem-
                       ber, if the steps are incomplete or too large, then there is
                       a higher probability that the training will be unsuccessful.

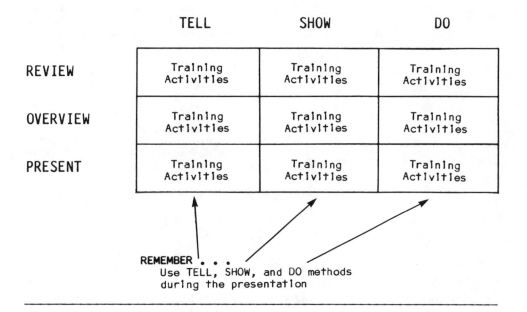

Example   Table 11, at the completion of this step, illustrates sample
                       presentation activities.

Substep 4:   The fourth substep is to develop training exercises.
  Develop   Training recipients need an opportunity to practice the
  Exercise   steps.   Training recipients should first perform each step
  Activities   by itself.   After the step has been acquired, then the
                       trainees should practice using the step in conjunction with
                       other steps.   The exercises should systematically lead to
                       applications of the steps in situations that are increas-
                       ingly similar to the work setting.   The more variable the
                       application exercises, the greater the probability that the
                       learning will be generalized and transferred.

                                                   Continued . . .

Substep 4:
  Develop
  Exercise
  Activities
  (Continued)

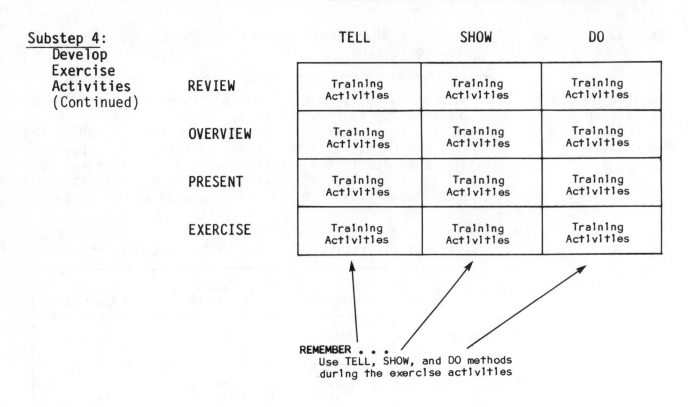

Example

Table 12, at the completion of this step, presents sample exercise activities.

Substep 5:
  Develop
  Summary
  Activities

The final substep is to develop summary activities. The summary activities answer the question: "What have the training recipients learned?" The summary is an index of our instruction as well as the trainees' learning.

Continued . . .

Substep 5:
  Develop
  Summary
  Activities
  (Continued)

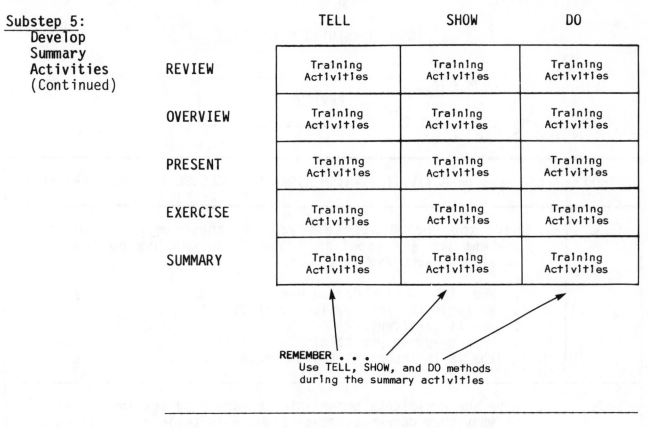

	TELL	SHOW	DO
REVIEW	Training Activities	Training Activities	Training Activities
OVERVIEW	Training Activities	Training Activities	Training Activities
PRESENT	Training Activities	Training Activities	Training Activities
EXERCISE	Training Activities	Training Activities	Training Activities
SUMMARY	Training Activities	Training Activities	Training Activities

REMEMBER . . .
Use TELL, SHOW, and DO methods
during the summary activities

Example   Table 13 presents sample summary activities.

Table 9.

SAMPLE TRAINING ACTIVITIES

```
┌──────────────────────────────────────────┐
│                  REVIEW                    │
└──────────────────────────────────────────┘
```

METHOD	EXAMPLES OF ACTIVITIES WHICH MIGHT BE INCLUDED IN A DELIVERY PLAN
TELL	• Have the recipients tell you how they currently do the content you are about to teach. You can use open-ended questions, such as: • What information do you need? • Where is the information located? • Who is involved? • What steps do you take? • Why is it important to take each step?
SHOW	• Have the recipients bring into the training session examples of what they currenty use or produce in their work settings.
DO	• Have the recipients do the procedures in a pre-training test or demonstration.

Table 10.

SAMPLE OVERVIEW ACTIVITIES

```
┌─────────────────────────────────────┐
│              OVERVIEW                │
└─────────────────────────────────────┘
```

METHOD	EXAMPLES OF ACTIVITIES WHICH MIGHT BE INCLUDED IN A DELIVERY PLAN
TELL	• Summarize the procedures currently being used. List these procedures on a flip chart. • Next, present the skill steps you are about to teach. • Compare the lists. Point out the similarities and differences between the lists. • Work with the recipients to consolidate the lists. These are the skill steps to be taught. • Ask the recipients where they are in relation to those skill steps. • Verbally reflect the recipients' input. • Give your perspective about the recipients' skill levels if there is a discrepancy between their images and the results of the pre-training test.
SHOW	• Together with the recipients, demonstrate the skill steps they are about to learn.
DO	• Ask the recipients to write down how they might use the skill steps in their work settings.

Table 11.

SAMPLE PRESENTATION ACTIVITIES

```
+------------------------------------------+
|               PRESENTATION               |
+------------------------------------------+
```

METHOD	EXAMPLES OF ACTIVITIES WHICH MIGHT BE INCLUDED IN A DELIVERY PLAN
TELL	• Present supportive knowledge: 　• What the step is_____ 　• What the step does_____(if - then)_____ 　• Why it is important_____(if - then - so that)_____ • Present the steps and substeps.
SHOW	• Show examples to illustrate the importance of using the steps and substeps. • Demonstrate the steps and substeps.
DO	• Have the recipients demonstrate the steps and substeps.

Table 12.

SAMPLE EXERCISE ACTIVITIES

EXERCISE

METHOD	EXAMPLES OF ACTIVITIES WHICH MIGHT BE INCLUDED IN A DELIVERY PLAN
TELL	• Have the recipients present the supportive knowledge and steps to each other.
SHOW	• Have the recipients demonstrate that they can do the steps under a supervised exercise.
DO	• Have the recipients repeat the exercise with less and less supervision. (REPEAT) • Have the recipients do the steps in an exercise which is a simulation of their work settings. Use the conditions and standards which are identified in the training objective to structure the simulation. (APPLY)

Table 13.

SAMPLE SUMMARY ACTIVITIES

┌─────────────────────┐
│   SUMMARY   │
└─────────────────────┘

METHOD	EXAMPLES OF ACTIVITIES WHICH MIGHT BE INCLUDED IN A DELIVERY PLAN
TELL	• Have the recipients summarize their learnings. • Have the recipients present, in summary fashion, the supportive knowledge and steps.
SHOW	• Have the recipients demonstrate how they will use the steps in their work settings.
DO	• Have the recipients develop a job aid for use in their work settings. • Have the recipients develop a follow-up plan to specify how they will implement the steps in their work settings. • Have the recipients complete a post-training assessment.

STEP 2: SELECT TRAINING MEDIA

What Are Training Media?

As stated previously, training media are the vehicles used for delivering the training content. Training media are selected for each training activity developed in Step 1.

Why Is The Selection Of Training Media Important?

This packaging of our training content can be a time-consuming and costly undertaking. Mistakes in media selection can affect both sides of the productivity goal. The wrong media selection can increase resource inputs while decreasing potential results outputs.

$$\frac{\text{RESULTS OUTPUTS } \downarrow}{\text{RESOURCE INPUTS } \uparrow}$$

WRONG MEDIA SELECTION

However, when the right training media are selected, they positively affect the productivity goal.

$$\frac{\text{RESULTS OUTPUTS } \uparrow}{\text{RESOURCE INPUTS } \downarrow}$$

RIGHT MEDIA SELECTION

What Types Of Media Can Be Selected?

Table 14 on the following page presents the most common training media used to present the TELL, SHOW, DO training activities.

Table 14.

SELECTING TRAINING MEDIA

MEDIA CATEGORY	MEDIA TECHNIQUE	WHEN TO USE . . .		
		TELL	SHOW	DO
AUDIO	• Audiotape • Audio Disc • Teleconference	✓ ✓ ✓		
AUDIO-VISUAL	• Film • Video • Video Disc • Video Conference • Video (Playback)	✓ ✓ ✓ ✓ ✓	✓ ✓ ✓ ✓ ✓	 ✓ ✓ ✓
COMPUTERS	• Drill and Practice • Simulation • Tutorials	 ✓	 ✓ ✓	✓ ✓ ✓
HUMAN RESOURCES	• Case Studies • Group Discussions • Internships • Field Trips • Lecture • Role Play	 ✓ ✓ ✓ 	✓ ✓ ✓ ✓	✓ ✓ ✓ ✓
MOTION-VISUAL	• Silent Films		✓	
OBJECTS	• Real Objects • Simulations		✓ ✓	✓ ✓
PRINT MATERIALS	• Charts • Flip Charts • Handouts • Job Aids • Manuals • Programmed Text	✓ ✓ ✓ ✓ ✓ ✓	 ✓ ✓ ✓ ✓	 ✓ ✓
PROJECTED STILL-VISUAL	• Slides • Film Strips • Transparencies	✓ ✓ ✓	✓ ✓ ✓	

**How Are Training
Media Selected?**

The following substeps are completed when selecting media:

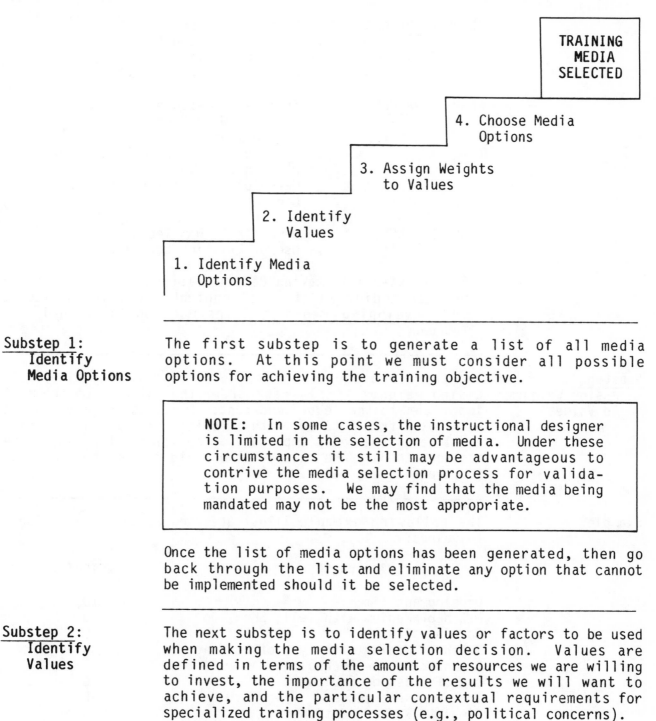

**Substep 1:
   Identify
   Media Options**

The first substep is to generate a list of all media options. At this point we must consider all possible options for achieving the training objective.

> **NOTE:** In some cases, the instructional designer is limited in the selection of media. Under these circumstances it still may be advantageous to contrive the media selection process for validation purposes. We may find that the media being mandated may not be the most appropriate.

Once the list of media options has been generated, then go back through the list and eliminate any option that cannot be implemented should it be selected.

**Substep 2:
   Identify
   Values**

The next substep is to identify values or factors to be used when making the media selection decision. Values are defined in terms of the amount of resources we are willing to invest, the importance of the results we will want to achieve, and the particular contextual requirements for specialized training processes (e.g., political concerns).

Example

Following are examples of values which typically enter into the media selection decision.

RESOURCE VALUES:
- Cost per Student
- Cost/Ease of Updating
- Development Time
- Practicality of Production

RESULTS VALUES:
- Trainee Preferences
- Simulate Work Conditions and Environments
- Match of Medium with Tell, Show, Do Methods
- Match of Medium* with Type of Content

PROCESS VALUES:
- Demonstrate New Technology
- Use of Existing Equipment

* For assistance in making determinations about the match between medium and type of content, refer to Selecting and Developing Media for Instruction, by Ronald H. Andrew.

Substep 3:
Assign Weights
To Values

The third substep is to assign weights to the values. To assign weights simply rank order the values from the most important to the least important. Next, assign a weight to each value from 1 to 10, with 10 being the most important, and 1 being the least important. The weight of 10 should be assigned to only one value. Other weights can be assigned to more than one value.

Example

The following example illustrates how weights are assigned to values:

VALUES	WEIGHT
Development Time	10
Match of Medium with Tell, Show, Do	9
Cost per Student	9
Match of Medium with Type of Content	8
Demonstrate New Technology	7
Use of Existing Equipment	6
Trainee Preferences	5
Simulate Work Conditions	3
Cost/Ease of Updating	2
Practicality of Production	1

Substep 4:
  Choose Media
  Options

The final substep is to choose the most preferable medium or media. To do this, we evaluate each media option in terms of the values.

		OPTIONS					
VALUES	**W**	**A**	**B**	**C**	**D**	**E**	**F**
A	(10)	++ (+20)	-- (-20)	0 (0)	+ (10)	- (-10)	0 (0)
B	(9)	- (- 9)	+ (+ 9)	++ (+18)	0 (0)	-- (-18)	+ (+ 9)
C	(8)	++ (+16)	+ (+ 8)	+ (+ 8)	- (- 8)	-- (-16)	0 (0)
D	(5)	++ (+10)	++(+10)	-- (-10)	0 (0)	+ (+ 5)	++ (+10)
E	(1)	0 (0)	-- (- 2)	++ (+ 2)	++ (+ 2)	- (- 1)	+ (+ 1)
TOTAL		37	5	18	4	-40	20

↑
MOST
PREFERABLE
OPTION

To complete the decision-making matrix:

1. Evaluate each media option against each value. Assign the following ratings:

    + + Medium Highly Likely to Meet Value
    +   Medium Likely to Meet Value
    0   Medium Neutral
    -   Medium Unlikely to Meet Value
    - - Medium Highly Unlikely to Meet Value

2. Multiply the weight of the value by the rating received.

    + + = 2
    + = 1
    0 = 0
    - = -1
    - - = -2

3. Total each column. The medium receiving the highest score is the most preferable selection.

Example

Table 15 presents an example of how media are selected.

155

PLANNING TRAINING DELIVERY
STEP 2: SELECT TRAINING MEDIA

Table 15.

EXAMPLE OF SELECTING TRAINING MEDIA

VALUES	WEIGHTS	INTERACTIVE VIDEO DISC	COMPUTER-BASED DRILL & PRACTICE	COMPUTER-BASED SIMULATION	VIDEO TAPE	PRINT JOB AID	PRINT PROGRAMMED TEXT	LECTURE	CASE STUDIES
Development Time	(10)	-- (-20)	-- (-20)	-- (-20)	-- (-20)	++ (+20)	+ (+10)	++ (+20)	+ (+10)
Match of Medium w/Tell, Show, Do	(9)	+ (+ 9)	++ (+18)	+ (+ 9)	+ (+ 9)	+ (+ 9)	+ (+ 9)	+ (+ 9)	- (- 9)
Cost per Student	(9)	-- (-18)	- (- 9)	-- (-18)	- (- 9)	++ (+18)	+ (+ 9)	+ (+ 9)	++ (+18)
Match of Medium w/Content Type	(8)	+ (+ 8)	++ (+16)	+ (+ 8)	- (- 8)	+ (+ 8)	+ (+ 8)	0 (0)	0 (0)
Demonstrate New Technology	(7)	++ (+14)	++ (+14)	++ (+14)	0 (0)	0 (0)	0 (0)	-- (-14)	-- (-14)
Use of Existing Equipment	(6)	-- (-12)	++ (+12)	++ (+12)	+ (+ 6)	- (- 6)	- (- 6)	- (- 6)	- (- 6)
Trainee Preferences	(5)	++ (+10)	++ (+10)	++ (+10)	+ (+ 5)	+ (+ 5)	-- (-10)	- (- 5)	0 (0)
Simulate Work Conditions	(3)	++ (+ 6)	0 (0)	++ (+ 6)	0 (0)	+ (+ 3)	0 (0)	- (- 3)	+ (+ 3)
Cost/Ease of Updating	(2)	-- (- 4)	-- (- 4)	-- (- 4)	-- (- 4)	++ (+ 4)	++ (+ 4)	++ (+ 4)	+ (+ 2)
Practicality of Production	(1)	-- (- 2)	-- (- 2)	-- (- 2)	-- (- 2)	++ (+ 2)	++ (+ 2)	++ (+ 2)	++ (+ 2)
TOTAL		- 9	35	15	-23	63	26	16	6

← THIS IS THE PREFERRED MEDIUM

NOTE: The instructional designer decided that the top three scoring media would be selected. The course was designed to include: computer-based drill and practice, print job aids, and print programmed text.

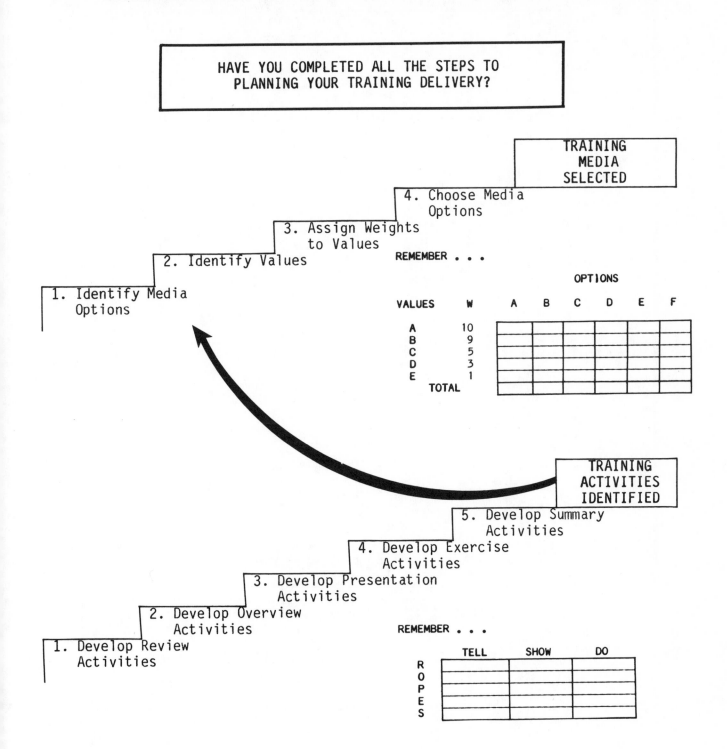

HAVE YOU COMPLETED ALL THE STEPS TO
PLANNING YOUR TRAINING DELIVERY?

TRAINING
MEDIA
SELECTED

4. Choose Media
   Options

3. Assign Weights
   to Values

2. Identify Values

1. Identify Media
   Options

REMEMBER . . .

OPTIONS

VALUES	W	A	B	C	D	E	F
A	10						
B	9						
C	5						
D	3						
E	1						
TOTAL							

TRAINING
ACTIVITIES
IDENTIFIED

5. Develop Summary
   Activities

4. Develop Exercise
   Activities

3. Develop Presentation
   Activities

2. Develop Overview
   Activities

1. Develop Review
   Activities

REMEMBER . . .

	TELL	SHOW	DO
R			
O			
P			
E			
S			

PLANNING TRAINING DELIVERY

Job Aids

JOB AID

DEVELOPING TRAINING DELIVERY PLAN

SUMMARY OF TRAINING OBJECTIVE: _____

PHASE OF DELIVERY: □ REVIEW □ OVERVIEW □ PRESENTATION □ EXERCISE □ SUMMARY

METHOD	DESCRIPTION OF TRAINING ACTIVITIES	MEDIA
TELL		
SHOW		
DO		

DEVELOPING TRAINING DELIVERY PLAN

SUMMARY OF TRAINING OBJECTIVE: __Making Work Assignments__

PHASE OF DELIVERY: ☐ REVIEW ☐ OVERVIEW ☑ PRESENTATION ☐ EXERCISE ☐ SUMMARY

METHOD	DESCRIPTION OF TRAINING ACTIVITIES	MEDIA
TELL	• Present the steps and substeps of making assignments. Have group identify principles. Add any that the group fails to mention. • Add facts and concepts used when making assignments.	Lecture Transparency Lecture
SHOW	• Show videotaped demonstration of the steps of making work assignments. • Demonstrate each substep using trainees in role play situations.	Video Role Play

Indicate the media to be used.

Describe the train-ing activity.

Indicate the phase of delivery. A job aid should be developed for each phase.

Summarize the components and functions of the training objective.

MAKING MEDIA SELECTION DECISIONS

	WEIGHTS							
VALUES								
TOTAL								

NOTE: See Table 15 for a completed example of the decision-making matrix.

SAMPLE LESSON PLANS

SAMPLE LESSON PLAN

KEY POINTS	LESSON PLAN	RESOURCES/TIME
	REVIEW	
		10 MINUTES
Group recalls experience with contracting	● INTRODUCTORY EXPERIENCE	
	- Tell the group to think about a contract they personally entered into (for example: to buy a house, lease an apartment, get a loan, etc.).	
Group answers questions on functions, components, and processes	- Ask the group to think about this contract when answering the following questions:	Write questions on flipchart
	1. What were the main reasons for having a contract? (FUNCTIONS)	
	2. What were the most important items included in the contract? (COMPONENTS)	
	3. What did you do before and after signing the contract? (PROCESSES)	
	- Have each participant complete Handout Intro. 2.	Handout Intro. 1, INTRODUCTORY EXERCISE
Group shares answers	- Ask the group to share their answers. Record the answers on a flipchart. Organize the answers into three columns labeled "Functions," "Components," and "Processes."	Record answers on flipchart
Add any missing functions, components and processes	- Add any functions, components, or processes not mentioned by the group.	

SAMPLE LESSON PLAN

| | OVERVIEW | |

KEY POINTS	LESSON PLAN	RESOURCES/TIME
		5 MINUTES
	• MATCHING IMAGES	
Note link between their personal experience and course content	- Stress that the introductory experience shows that they are familiar with the basic functions, components, and processes used in contracting. Indicate that this course will focus on the use of these skills and knowledge in procurement and assistance.	
Get group's input	- Ask the group what they hope to learn from the training. Record responses on flipchart.	Record responses on flipchart
Relate group's needs to training agenda	- Review the training agenda and course objectives. Point out content areas that address the concerns expressed by the group. If possible, adjust the agenda to emphasize the group's objectives.	Handout Intro. 2, TRAINING AGENDA
Address areas not covered	- Explain how they can get information on areas of interest not covered during the training.	

SAMPLE LESSON PLAN

PRESENTATION

KEY POINTS	LESSON PLAN	RESOURCES/TIME
	• **THE WHY'S BEHIND THE REGULATIONS**	10 MINUTES
Complexity of regulations	– Explain that most individuals consider procurement and acquisition regulations to be rather massive and complex.	
Get group's input on principles behind regulations	– Ask the group what they think are the basic intentions of the acquisition and assistance regulations.	
	NOTE: Make sure the responses are principles. Principles include a "so that" statement. If a participant's response is not a principle, ask the "so that" question.	
	– Record the group's answers on a flipchart using two columns. Put all responses dealing with the protection of the Government's interests in one column. In the second column, record all responses that relate to protecting the public's interests.	Record answers on flipchart
Tell group major principles	– Review Transparency 1.2 and tell the group that the principles underlying acquisition and assistance regulations are:	Transparency 1.2, FOUNDATION OF ACQUISITION AND ASSISTANCE POLICY AND REGULATIONS
	1. The protection of the Government's interests. 2. The protection of the public's interests.	

EXERCISE

KEY POINTS	LESSON PLAN	RESOURCES/TIME
Exercise on problem identification	**• EXERCISE** – Ask the participants to read the case study presented in Handout 3.4. Divide the participants into groups. Ask each group to discuss the case study and to: • Identify the indicators of the performance problem. • Establish the contractor's current and expected levels of performance. • Estimate the impact of the problem on the entire contract and on the agency. – Request that each group record their responses on a flipchart. – Bring the group back together. Review and discuss each group's responses. **NOTE:** If there are discrepancies among the groups, discuss the reasons for the differing perspectives.	**15 MINUTES** Handout 3.4, CASE STUDY, PART 1

SAMPLE LESSON PLAN

SUMMARY

KEY POINTS	LESSON PLAN	RESOURCES/TIME
		10 MINUTES
Ask group to summarize learnings	• UNIT SUMMARY - Ask the group to write down the three most important points they learned and how each point relates to their work tasks. - Have the group share their learning. NOTE: If this activity fails to give you an accurate index of the group's learning then you may want to administer a unit post-test.	
Respond to questions	- Ask if there are any questions before you move to Unit 2: Pre-Award Phase.	Record responses on flipchart

SUMMARY

Our Choice

Basically, we have two choices. We can continue on our past course of consuming resources and randomly impacting the performance results. Or, we can choose to be productive through programmatic interventions.

Summary: Designing Productive Interventions

Remember, a productive intervention design includes:

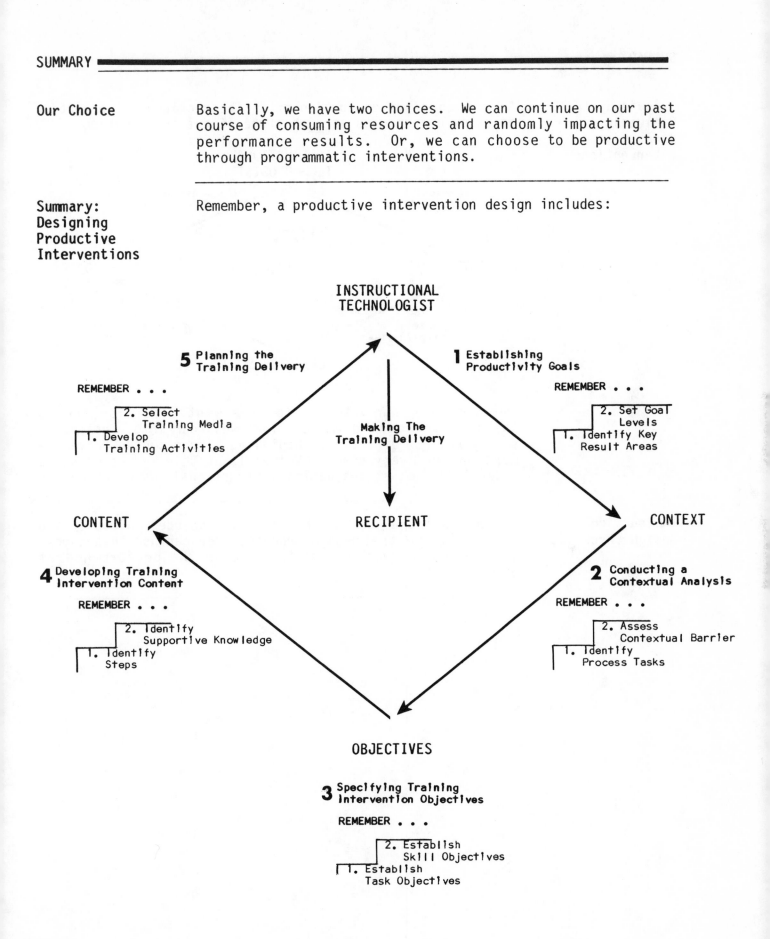

INSTRUCTIONAL TECHNOLOGIST

5 Planning the Training Delivery

REMEMBER . . .

2. Select Training Media
1. Develop Training Activities

Making The Training Delivery

1 Establishing Productivity Goals

REMEMBER . . .

2. Set Goal Levels
1. Identify Key Result Areas

CONTENT

RECIPIENT

CONTEXT

4 Developing Training Intervention Content

REMEMBER . . .

2. Identify Supportive Knowledge
1. Identify Steps

2 Conducting a Contextual Analysis

REMEMBER . . .

2. Assess Contextual Barrier
1. Identify Process Tasks

OBJECTIVES

3 Specifying Training Intervention Objectives

REMEMBER . . .

2. Establish Skill Objectives
1. Establish Task Objectives

**Overview:
Evaluating
Productive
Interventions**

A comprehensive evaluation of an instructional intervention assesses our results at <u>each</u> stage of the intervention.

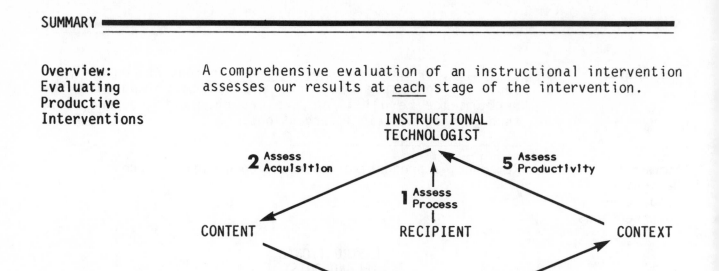

When designing our intervention, we went clockwise around the instructional diamond. To assess our intervention, we simply reverse directions, beginning at the content development and delivery stage. Volume II of this series presents a detailed look at evaluating instructional intervention.

**Instructional
Design Checklist**

An instructional design checklist is included to assist you in monitoring the design process. You can use this checklist to monitor your own performance or the performance of others.

┌───┐
│   ESTABLISHING PRODUCTIVITY GOALS   │
└───┘

COMPLETED?

IDENTIFY KEY RESULT AREAS

    1.   Review Productivity Mission   ☐
    2.   Identify Organizational Components/Units   ☐
    3.   Identify Inputs, Processes, and Outputs   ☐
    4.   Select Key Result Areas   ☐

SET GOAL LEVELS

    1.   Determine Current Results Outputs   ☐
    2.   Determine Current Resource Inputs   ☐
    3.   Establish Desired Results Outputs   ☐
    4.   Establish Desired Resource Inputs   ☐

┌───┐
│   ANALYZING CONTEXTUAL TASKS   │
└───┘

IDENTIFY PROCESS TASKS

    1.   Identify Delivery Tasks   ☐
    2.   Identify Supervisory Tasks   ☐
    3.   Identify Management Tasks   ☐

ASSESS CONTEXTUAL BARRIERS

    1.   Identify Delivery-Level Barriers   ☐
    2.   Continue Barrier Analysis (If Needed)   ☐

SPECIFYING TRAINING OBJECTIVES

COMPLETED?

ESTABLISH TASK OBJECTIVES

1.	Select Tasks	☐
2.	Define Components	☐
3.	Define Functions	☐
4.	Define Processes	☐
5.	Define Conditions	☐
6.	Define Standards	☐

ESTABLISH SKILL OBJECTIVES

1.	Determine Need for Skill Objectives	☐
2.	Identify Skill Areas	☐
3.	Define Components	☐
4.	Define Functions	☐
5.	Define Processes	☐
6.	Define Conditions	☐
7.	Define Standards	☐

DEVELOPING TRAINING CONTENT

IDENTIFY STEPS

1.	Identify DO Steps	☐
2.	Identify DO Substeps	☐
3.	Identify THINK Steps	☐

IDENTIFY SUPPORTIVE KNOWLEDGE

1.	Identify Facts	☐
2.	Identify Concepts	☐
3.	Identify Principles	☐

PLANNING TRAINING DELIVERY

COMPLETED?

DEVELOP TRAINING ACTIVITIES

1.	Develop Review Activities	☐
2.	Develop Overview Activities	☐
3.	Develop Presentation Activities	☐
4.	Develop Exercise Activities	☐
5.	Develop Summary Activities	☐

SELECT TRAINING MEDIA

1.	Identify Media Options	☐
2.	Identify Values	☐
3.	Assign Weights to Values	☐
4.	Choose Media Options	☐

GLOSSARY

Application Evaluation: An assessment that measures whether or not training recipients can use the training content in work simulations.

Acquisition Evaluation: An assessment that measures whether or not training recipients have acquired the training content.

Components: Nouns in a training objective which describe persons, data, or things involved in performing the task/skill behavior ("who").

Concepts: Descriptions of how the various facts affect one another, often expressed in cause-and-effect relationships ("If. . ., then. . .").

Conditions: Adverbial phrases in a training objective describing the context in which the behavior takes place ("where"), the timeline for performing the behavior ("when"), and the purposes to be achieved by performing the behavior ("why").

Consulting Intervention: An intervention with the purpose of refining the productivity mission so that strategic plans can be developed.

Content: The steps, substeps, and supportive knowledge to be delivered to training recipients.

Content Development: Identification of the steps and knowledge required to achieve the training objectives.

Context: The work environment in which the recipients will be expected to perform task or skill behaviors.

Contextual Barriers: Any source which prevents the performance of the process tasks.

Contextual Tasks: The groups of work activities that must be performed to achieve the productivity goals.

Delivery Plan: The training activities, methods, and media to be used for ensuring the effective delivery of the training content.

Do: Training method that provides recipients with the opportunity to actually do the task/skill behavior.

DO Steps: The major steps the trainees will need to do to perform the task or skill.

DO Substeps: Sub-behaviors which, when added together, will lead to the performance of a DO step.

Enabling Task: A task necessary to support a process task.

Exercise: Element of content organization in which the training recipients practice the tasks or skills.

Facts: The components, functions, and processes of the training objective or step.

Functions: Verbs in a training objective which describe the desired behavioral outcomes of the instructional intervention ("what").

Goal Level: Determination of the amount of change desired to occur in a key result area as a result of the training intervention.

Inputs: People, information, and/or capital resources which are used to accomplish the productivity mission.

Intervention: The process of initiating change.

Key Result Areas: The few organizational outputs that are critical to the achievement of the productivity mission.

Media: Vehicles or methods trainers use to deliver training content.

Organizational Components: The resource, production, marketing, and distribution segments of the organization.

Outputs: The finished products, services, and/or benefits resulting from the achievement of a goal.

Overview: Element of content organization in which images are shared with the training recipients on the content and its importance.

Preferred Courses of Action: The courses of action which maximize the probability of achieving strategic goals while minimizing the costs.

Presentation: Element of content organization in which content is presented so that recipients can learn the tasks or skills and accomplish the training objectives.

Principles: Descriptions of how and why something works, usually dealing with the implications of the cause-and-effect relationships of the concepts ("If. . ., then. . ., so that. . .").

Processes: Adverbial phrases that modify the functions of a training objective to describe the means by which the task/skill behavior is performed to reach the desired outcome ("how").

Process Tasks: The groups of work activities that must be performed by delivery, supervisory, and management personnel to achieve the productivity goals.

Productivity Achievement: The training recipients' achievement of productivity goals (i.e., the comparison of results outputs and resource inputs).

Productivity Evaluation: An assessment measuring the costs (inputs) and benefits (outputs) of a teaching intervention.

Productivity Goal: The desired outputs and anticipated levels of resource inputs.

Productivity Mission: A statement of goals for a target population, emphasizing a comparison of results outputs with resource inputs.

Programmatic: Step-by-step procedures to achieve desired goals.

Qualitative Goals: Desired outputs stated in terms of accuracy, functionality, or initiative.

Quantitative Goals: Desired outputs stated in terms of volume, rate, or timeliness.

Recipient: The individual who is to receive the training intervention.

Return-on-Investment (ROI): Ratio of the increments in results brought about by the added resource investments.

Review: Element of content organization in which content is reviewed in order to get an index of what the recipients do and do not know about the content to be addressed.

ROPES: Acronym for the content organization elements of Review, Overview, Presentation, Exercise, and Summary.

Show: Training method that demonstrates to the recipients how to do the task/skill behavior.

Skill Objectives: Those objectives that focus on the skills or behavioral objectives underlying the performance of contextual tasks.

Skills: Observable and repeatable behavior.

Standards: Adverbial phrases in a training objective which describe, in absolute or relative terms, the desired level of excellence to be achieved in performing the task ("how well").

Steps: Those behaviors which, when added together, will lead to the accomplishment of the training objectives.

Strategic Components: The organizational units which share in the achievement of the mission.

Strategic Delivery: The presentation of the strategic plans to decision makers, during which the decision makers process and refine the plans.

Strategic Goals: Goals which support the achievement of a productivity mission.

Strategic Plans: Designs for implementing the preferred courses of action that enable the organization to achieve the strategic goals and the productivity mission.

Substeps: Those sub-behaviors which, when added together, will lead to the performance of a task/skill step.

Summary: Element of content organization in which content is summarized in order to get an index of what the recipients do and do not know about the tasks or skills following the training delivery.

Supportive Knowledge: Facts, concepts, and principles which are needed in order to perform a task or skill.

Task Objectives: Those objectives that focus primarily on the performance of specific contextual tasks.

Tell: Training method that informs the recipients about what task/skill behavior is to be done and how to do it.

THINK Steps: Questions for training recipients to answer before, during, and after completing a DO step or substep so they can monitor their own performance.

Training Delivery Plan: Vehicle used by the instructional technologist to provide training recipients with new tasks, skills, and knowledge. A training delivery plan organizes the content, establishes the training methods, and specifies the training media.

Training Methods: Didactic (tell), modeling (show), and exercise (do).

Transfer Evaluation: An assessment which measures whether or not training recipients use the training content (skills/knowledge) in the performance of their jobs.